SEW AND SAVE

JOANNA CHASE

Gives expert help with the problems of clothes care,
renovations, war-time dressmaking, and rationing.
Includes knitting patterns, and a four-year plan
for the family wardrobe. Illustrated.

Harper
Press

Harper*Press*
An imprint of HarperCollins*Publishers*
77–85 Fulham Palace Road
Hammersmith, London W6 8JB
www.harpercollins.co.uk

Visit our authors' blog: www.fifthestate.co.uk
Love this book? www.bookarmy.com

First published in Great Britain by
The Literary Press Ltd, Glasgow, in 1941
This edition was first published by Harper*Press* in 2009

1

A catalogue record for this book is available from the British Library

ISBN 978-0-00-731377-8

Printed and bound in Great Britain by Clays Ltd, St Ives plc

CONTENTS

FROCKS, BLOUSES AND SKIRTS

TRICKS FOR SMARTNESS

ACCESSORIES COSTING
NEXT-TO-NOTHING

MAKE MORE OF OLD CLOTHES

DRESSING THE CHILDREN

IDEAS FOR HATS

SERVICE AND FAMILY WOOLLIES

ILLUSTRATIONS

TO PLAN YOUR WARDROBE

EVERY woman wants to be well dressed. At any time, but especially in war-time, and now that clothes are rationed, this is a matter of planning rather than of plenty. So find five minutes to sit down with a piece of paper and pencil and plan your wardrobe carefully to fit in with the money you have to spend and the type of life you lead. Go over your existing clothes and make a list of what is still wearable, what will have to be replaced, and your next necessary and important " buys."

When you've done that decide on a colour scheme and stick to it, otherwise you'll find you have odd frocks that don't match your overcoat, or a sweater without a matching skirt, and not enough coupons to remedy these difficulties.

YOUR MOST IMPORTANT GARMENT

For any woman, be she housewife, world-worker, or both, the most important item in her wardrobe is her overcoat. It is worth while apportioning 15% of the money you have to spend on a good overcoat that will last you for several years. Remember that it is in your overcoat that you present yourself to the world, also that it has to keep you warm and therefore keep you well. Get a good one.

Choose a simple cut that will not date, and a closely-woven wool that will wear well and not pull out of shape. Forgo fur (which begins to look shabby while the rest of the coat is still good), and forgo " amusing " buttons that you will not be able to replace if you lose one.

Look for a tailored coat, semi-fitted, with high-buttoning neck-line and a slightly flared skirt. This type of coat remains in fashion for years. Or if you are plump and feel " bunched up " in a fitted topcoat, there is nothing to beat the tailored full-length swagger, as the full straight lines of this type of coat are slenderising, while the easy cut of raglan sleeves obviates any drag across broad shoulders or a full bust.

Choose a dark basic colour for your coat, black, navy, nigger or deep green. It is more economical, as it will then go with all your frocks, and you are also less likely to get tired of it.

A SUIT THAT WILL NOT DATE

The next most important item in the average wardrobe is a coat and skirt. This, too, if you choose a classic style, should last many years. The best type to buy has a fairly straight skirt with a box-pleat, about 8 inches wide, back and front for ease of movement, and a fitted tailored jacket with three buttons and high revers and lapels. It is wise to choose this in the same colour as your overcoat so that the same hat, shoes, bag and gloves will serve for both.

A suit is a boon to a woman who cannot have many clothes, for she can vary her appearance for every occasion on which she wears it with sweaters and blouses in different fabrics and colours. A black suit can be worn all through the winter with bright or pastel wool jumpers, which she can knit for herself for under five shillings, and when the spring comes she can make herself a muslin, silk or rayon blouse out of only two yards of material. Blouses, made from the same pattern in fine woollen stuffs, help the suit round again into early autumn.

Another economy point about a suit is that you can launder your jumpers and blouses at home, and save the money you would have to spend on cleaners' bills for frocks.

HOW TO BUY FROM A DRESS AGENCY

Now that we have clothes rationing with us, it is a very good plan to consider buying second-hand clothes. Clothes from the dress agencies normally cost about a quarter of their original price. They are all cleaned before being resold, and in any case have often only been very little worn by their original owners.

When you go to a dress agency, you should look at the underarms and the neck-line of anything you may choose. If these are worn you cannot do very much with them. If the fabric of the garment is good, don't let shabby trimmings worry you. Pockets, neck trimmings, missing buttons can all be replaced. You will not only save money this way, but often get a better-styled, better-made garment than a new one at the same price. This applies particularly to overcoats and suits.

FROCKS TO SUIT YOUR CIRCUMSTANCES

Besides these two items, the average woman should have two or three frocks in her wardrobe. Their cut and style, fabric and colour depend largely on the type of life she leads.

The housewife who goes out to tea with her neighbours, or with her husband to play cards in the evenings, will like to have patterned or soft-coloured materials, and a rather more fussy style than her sister who works in an office and prefers plain one-colour clothes. Again, the woman who lives in the country may find that frocks are of little use to her, and will make up her wardrobe with odd skirts, jumpers, and little jackets in different fabrics and colours that are interchangeable. There are, however, certain basic rules about style, fabric and colour that will help you not to make bad mistakes in your dressing.

CLOTHES FOR THE SHORT AND PLUMP

If you are short and plump, remember that light colours, bright colours, large prints and glossy fabrics make you look larger. Heavy, rough fabrics will add to your bulk. Thin, clinging materials reveal the shape beneath them. The plump woman should therefore choose one-colour fabrics with a dull surface in fine wool or heavy silk.

Large hips can be made to look smaller by wearing padded shoulder-lines. This helps to balance the figure. An illusion of height is given by wearing straight princess lines, unfussy bodices with vertical tucks or embroidery, longish skirts with high heels. Short women should wear their belts a little higher than their natural waist-lines to make their legs look longer. They should never wear boleros, wide belts, sashes or little fitted jackets, as these things cut the short woman in half and make her look dumpy. Pleats are better than gathers, large tailored tucks better than full drapery. All downward lines help to slenderise.

CLOTHES FOR THE TALL WOMAN

The tall, angular woman should never wear vertical stripes. She should bear in mind that heavy fabrics will give her bulk, that high halter neck-lines cover salt-cellars and a scraggy neck, full gathered bodices will make more of her bust, and wide flared or gathered skirts over narrow hips make for elegance and detract from gaucherie. Fabrics with a surface sheen help to give a rounded, curved look to the angular figure, while blouses and skirts in contrasting colours will cut her figure in half, and little fitted jackets worn with fairly short skirts will break the length of line.

The *petite*, slim woman is best off of all, as she can wear any style, any fabric, and any design *except large bold prints*. Big patterns on small people create the impression that there is a dress, and there *may* be a woman inside it.

TO CHOOSE AND BLEND COLOURS

The choice of colour for your clothes is largely a matter of personal preference, for no woman will feel well-dressed or happy in a colour she herself dislikes. Generally speaking, fair women look best in black, navy, grey, and all pastel colours. Brunettes can wear black, brown, green, and some of the lighter shades of grey. A fairly safe rule is for a dark woman to avoid colours containing any element of blue, which make the skin look sallow, and for a blonde to steer clear of the yellow and orange tones.

The blending of colours is another problem. With the exception of navy, you can put anything and everything with black. With navy, good colours are white, yellow, dusty pinks, pale blues, lavender and purple. With brown you can use yellow again, flame, rust, aquamarine blue, grass green, sage green and deep crimson. Grey is enlivened by white, yellow, nut-brown and emerald.

MAKING YOUR COUPONS GO ROUND

Now that clothes and dress materials are rationed, it is essential that every wardrobe should be carefully planned, no matter how little money matters to the wearer. Moreover, it is necessary to plan for several years ahead and not just from season to season as formerly. Unless planning is done well ahead, you may find yourself obliged to spend all your coupons on things like underwear and shoes when circumstances demand that you should have a new top garment.

In order to make your coupons go round you will, of course, make it a rule to buy the best garments you can afford, as far as durability of material is concerned. Even if your wardrobe already contains good and fairly new basic garments, you will be wise to spend your coupons on more of such garments now rather than in a year or two's time when the best material may no longer be available.

Another point to remember is that many of your existing garments can be made to serve in other capacities before their lives are finally over. Old evening-frocks, for instance, can be made over to blouses or to summer skirts or, if the material is too fragile for these purposes, to fine lingerie.

How you spend your coupons will naturally depend on your individual requirements, your purse, and any modifications in the ration that may be made from time to time. To help you choose the variations, however, here are two plans, one for a woman and one for a man, showing how replacements can be made to an existing stock of clothes to ensure a reasonable appearance during the next four years in spite of rationing.

In the plan for a woman, wool or material is included regularly because many women will prefer to make their own gloves, scarves, stockings, etc., rather than spend coupons on each of these small, but important accessories. The number of coupons required for each garment is not stated, in order to allow for future variations in the rations available.

FOUR-YEAR PLAN FOR A WOMAN'S WARDROBE

First Year.

1 pair shoes.
6 pairs stockings.
10 ozs. wool or 2½ yds. material.
1 suit.
1 overcoat.
2 slips.
1 blouse (home-made).

Third Year.

2 pairs shoes.
6 pairs stockings.
4 ozs. wool or 1 yd. material.
1 jacket.
1 skirt.
2 cotton or silk frocks.
2 slips.
1 pair corsets.

Second Year.

1 pair shoes.
6 pairs stockings.
8 ozs. wool or 2 yds. material.
1 silk dress.
Underwear :
  Cami-knickers or vest and
    knickers (2 or 3 pairs).
  Corselette or brassière and
    girdle (2 or 3 pairs)
6 handkerchiefs.

Fourth Year.

1 pair shoes.
6 pairs stockings.
6 ozs. wool or 1½ yds. material.
1 woollen housecoat or dressing-
    gown.
1 blouse.
Underwear :
  Cami-knickers or vest and
    knickers (2 or 3 pairs).
  Corselette or brassière and
    girdle (2 or 3 pairs).
6 handkerchiefs.

Evening-gowns are omitted from the plan since they are, in any case, not essential garments for most people. Special sportswear is also omitted on the same grounds. A mackintosh is not included because umbrellas, which are unrationed, can be made to serve instead, used in conjunction with an old coat.

FOUR-YEAR PLAN FOR A MAN'S WARDROBE

First Year.

1 pair boots or shoes.
6 pairs socks.
1 suit (no waistcoat).
1 overcoat.
Collars, tie or handkerchiefs.

Third Year.

1 pair boots or shoes.
5 pairs socks.
1 suit.
1 pullover.
2 pairs pyjamas.

Second Year.

1 pair boots or shoes.
6 pairs socks.
1 pair corduroy trousers.
3 shirts (silk or cotton).
2 pairs of pants.
2 vests.
1 pair gloves.

Fourth Year.

1 pair boots or shoes.
6 pairs socks.
1 overcoat, or unlined mackin-
    tosh and vests.
3 shirts.
2 pairs of pants.
Collars, ties or handkerchiefs.

TO EKE OUT CHILDREN'S RATIONS

How you plan your children's wardrobes will depend so much on the size and age of your family that no useful guide can be given. Your problems, difficult as they are, can nevertheless be eased in a number of ways. For instance, either through the school or through your local Women's Institute, you may be able to get in touch with other mothers and arrange to exchange your children's garments. You give a good dress or a suit, too small for your own daughter or son, and get in exchange a pair of shoes or a coat which can be worn for a year or more. Children notoriously dislike wearing one another's clothes, but the objection is not likely to be so strong if the clothes have belonged to unknown children living in other districts.

The question of school uniforms is already being tackled by the schools themselves. Uniforms are likely to be considerably simplified and, for the rest, an exchange system is almost certain to be worked out before the difficulties become formidable.

TAKE CARE OF YOUR CLOTHES

CLOTHES, like everything else in the world, respond to care and kindness in your treatment of them. If you look after them, they'll not only last you much longer but will retain indefinitely the speckless appearance they had when you bought them, thus giving you a well-groomed air which is more than half-way to being a well-dressed woman.

The secret of looking after clothes is to make a regular job of it, just like washing up or sweeping the drawing-room carpet. Allot a few hours one day each week to going over your wardrobe for cleaning and repairs.

TO WELCOME A NEW GARMENT

Start off by examining carefully any new clothes that you buy ready-made. See that things like press-studs, buckles and buttons are firmly sewn on to the garment. Look at the inside finishings of seams and hems, and if they are likely to fray, overcast them yourself. Sew dress protectors into a new frock. If the neck of a new blouse doesn't quite fit, alter the top fastening so that it does. Knot and cut off any stray pieces of thread that may have been left hanging loose in the finishing.

PRECAUTIONS IN PUTTING CLOTHES AWAY

When you are storing clothes, remember that all shoes should be wrapped in newspaper, and all dark or heavy garments folded with sheets of newspaper between them. The printers' ink is disliked by moth. Mothballs, of course, are an elementary precaution.

Summer clothes should be stored in white paper so that they do not get soiled; hats put crown downwards into large boxes, one crown into the next. If you are storing silk lingerie, or silk stockings that are new, do not wash them, but put them into an air-tight jar and seal the top. In this way they will keep without perishing.

A BED-TIME ROUTINE FOR CLOTHES

Your three great allies in clothes care are heat, steam and a good stiff brush. Always brush your clothes when you take them off at night, as dust left on overnight works its way into the material and is responsible for that grey "bloom" on clothes. Buy several twopenny wooden hangers, so that when you hang your clothes up they fall into their natural folds and

7

retain their shape. Be sure to get the hangers wide enough, so that the shoulders of clothes do not sag over the ends. Never hang a garment on a hook by its neck. If you do that, you simply ask for bulging neck-lines and sagging hems.

TO ARRANGE YOUR WARDROBE

Arrange the hanging space in your wardrobe or cupboard so that all the heavy dark-coloured things are together at one end, and the lighter, more delicate fabrics at the other. It is a good idea to make dust-proof covers for your clothes. They can easily be made from old sheeting. Cut a double piece of material straight down into an oblong about 30 inches wide, and the length of your dress. Seam up the sides, and slightly shape the top into a curve to fit over the shoulders of a hanger. You can do this by placing a hanger flat on the material and tracing round it. Seam up the shoulder-lines and leave an opening about a foot across at the top, so that the cover is easily slipped over your dresses.

Evening frocks should always be hung on double hangers, so that the skirt can be lifted off the floor of the wardrobe and hung through the rung of the hanger. This prevents dust and dirt collecting round the hem of a long skirt.

Skirts should always be hung on proper skirt hangers, which are similar to trouser hangers, and clip the skirt firmly across at the waist-line. The skirt should be folded in half, and care taken to see that the hem and waist are level ; it is then clipped flat into the hanger. This stops the waist-line from stretching or dropping. Skirt hangers cost from about a shilling each and are a good investment.

CARE FOR HATS AND SHOES

Hats should be brushed before they are put away, and preferably stood on hat-stands, which can be bought from most chain stores for about 4d. each. If, however, you haven't the space for hat-stands, always lay a hat down on its crown to prevent the brim taking the weight of the hat and curling into curious shapes. Hats should be covered with tissue paper when they are not in use.

Shoes should always be cleaned and put on trees when you take them off at night. Metal and wooden trees may be more and more difficult to get in war-time, but little balls of newspaper pushed down tightly into the shoe will do as well.

Brown shoes of good leather which have become stained can be gently scrubbed with saddle soap and a little tepid water, and will then come up like new. Black kid or glacé shoes that are wearing grey can be reconditioned by the application of a mixture of Indian ink (from 6d. a bottle) and olive oil. Patent leather shoes should *never* be brushed, but cleaned with milk and a soft rag. To brighten them try a drop of turpentine.

It is unwise to use a wire brush on suède shoes, as this will in time tear them. Use a rubber brush, and if the shoes become badly rubbed or grease-stained you can restore the nap by rubbing gently with fine emery paper.

To bring up a high polish on leather shoes of any description, rub over with a piece of soft, clean silk.

WHEN YOU'VE BEEN CAUGHT IN THE RAIN

If you get your shoes wet never dry them in front of a fire. Stuff them immediately with newspaper and leave them in a warm atmosphere. Don't attempt to polish them until they are quite dry.

All garments that get wet in the rain should be shaken out and hung on hangers in a warm atmosphere. Felt hats, coats and suits, velvet or shantung silk that have got spotted by rain should be steamed to remove the spots. Pass the affected parts of the garment rapidly to and fro in front of the escaping steam from the spout of a boiling kettle. This will remove the spots.

DON'T LET YOUR GLOVES GIVE YOU AWAY

Stained and shapeless gloves will give you away at once, yet nine women out of ten, when they take their gloves off, crumple them into a ball and throw them into the nearest drawer to hand. There is much to be said for the old-fashioned glove box that kept gloves flat. Keep them in an old chocolate box, or if you find boxes a nuisance, do at least smooth them out when you take them off and lay them flat at the bottom of a shallow drawer.

Don't let your gloves get to the state when they're past repair before you think about mending them. A split finger seam should be mended immediately. All gloves should be brushed well, or washed (in the case of light gloves) at least once a week when you do the rest of your laundry. Then they never get so grubby that they don't wash clean.

Hogskin gloves should be washed on the hands in tepid soapy water, then rinsed and wiped. Do not hang them up : blow into them until they take the shape of the hand, and leave them on a towel to dry.

Suède gloves can be brushed up with a rubber brush—you can get special glove rubbers for this for a few pence. If, however, they are badly soiled, immerse them in benzine or aviation petrol and squeeze out the dirt. Several lots of spirit should be used, until they are quite clean, then they should be dried with a soft cloth. Kid gloves also can be cleaned in this way. Generally speaking, where dark suède or kid gloves are concerned, it is wiser to send them to the cleaners, as sometimes the spirit is apt to remove the colour and they come up patchy. Professional cleaners have methods of re-dyeing gloves to get over this difficulty. They charge between 1/- and 1/6 a pair.

Many people like to use glove stretchers to dry their gloves on after washing or cleaning. Personally, I think these sometimes force a glove out of the shape it has already taken on the hand, and are apt to stretch it too much. Blowing into gloves is a better way of keeping their shape. However, it is a matter of opinion, and glove stretchers can be bought at any draper's shop for a shilling or two a pair.

BANISHING SPOTS AND "TIREDNESS" IN CLOTHES

A black frock or coat that has become rather dusty-looking can be restored at home by sponging with cold tea. Grease spots can be removed by putting the affected part between two sheets of clean blotting paper and pressing firmly with a hot iron. If the spot doesn't come out with the first pressing, use fresh blotting paper. If you try to move the blotting paper, you may press the grease it has already absorbed back into another part of the frock.

Bad grease stains are often removable at home by rubbing with magnesia, taking care to cover the stain completely, and then pressing next day with a hot iron. If the stain is still stubborn, there are many inexpensive patent removers on the market which will do the trick.

Grease stains on the neck-lines of suits and coats, and in the rims of hats, can be removed by brushing with a clean brush dipped in a pint of warm water in which you have put a teaspoonful of ammonia. When the grease has been removed rub with a clean, dry cloth.

Shine from the back of skirts, elbows and wrists of coats is often removable with a solution of a teaspoonful of alum and a teaspoonful of strong ammonia in a pint of warm water. Be careful not to make the garment too wet. On very thick serges shine can be dealt with by rubbing over gently with emery paper and then brushing with a stiff brush. Don't rub too hard or you'll wear a hole in the fabric.

WHEN CLEANING LEAVES A RING BEHIND

A common sequence to removing grease stains is "rings" on the patch you've been trying to clean. This is usually because too much dampness has been applied to the stain, or it has been allowed to spread by not drying the spot thoroughly afterwards with a clean cloth. When this happens you can either start again and take care to dry the mark thoroughly, or remove the ring with a clean cloth and a little methylated spirit. If you're still uncertain of your touch in applying the cleaning agent, put it into a sixpenny scent or shampoo spray, and spray it on to the stain or " ring."

FURS REPAY SPECIAL CARE

Each time furs are taken off they should be shaken, and the hairs smoothed down with the hand before they are put away. If you have a line in the garden, hang your fur out on a dry windy day. This will help to keep fur clean by blowing the dust out of it, and also to retain its thick and glossy appearance.

If fur gets wet in the rain, it should be wiped with a cloth and hung up to dry in a warm atmosphere, but not near a fire as this hardens the skin by shrinking it.

To clean furs they should be laid out flat on a table and sprinkled with warm bran or Fuller's earth. Separate the hairs with your fingers and rub the bran in gently with a clean, dry cloth. Leave it overnight, and then shake out well in the morning, and beat the back of the pelt with a thin cane. You should be able to clean the fur completely this way, but if any particles of bran remain, blow on the fur, or a pair of bellows, if you have them, will do the job less breathlessly.

POINTS TO REMEMBER WHEN IRONING

Pressing and ironing are matters in which every woman will have her own pet tricks by which she swears. If you are doubtful about ironing on the right or wrong side of material, remember that the rule is to iron on the right side of the material if you want a shiny finish, and on the wrong side for a dull one.

Linen, thick heavy woollens, and cottons need a fairly hot iron. Silk, any kind of artificial silk, and lace, need cool irons. Cotton, linen and woollens can be damped before ironing. Silk, artificial silk and lace, however, should never be damped once they have dried or they will iron up patchy. The secret is to squeeze as much water as you can out of them after washing, and then iron them before they are completely dry. A good rule is to iron them two hours after you have hung them up to dry. Tussore silk should be ironed bone dry. If you iron it wet, it will become paper-stiff and there's nothing you can do about it.

TIPS ON WASHING KNITTED THINGS

Jumpers and any kind of knitted silk or wool underwear need careful handling in laundering if they are to keep their shape. The best method I have found so far for doing this is to tack the garment when it needs washing to a thin piece of towelling. Take special care to tack the neck-line and sleeves firmly, also the waist-line. Then wash the whole thing gently, including the towel, by squeezing till all the dirt is out. It is wise to keep a couple of bowls of water on hand when washing garments of this description, then you can lift them direct from one basin to the next on your hands and the weight of water does not pull them out of shape. These precautions may seem a lot of trouble if you have a pile of laundering to do, but garments will keep their shape this way, and by preventing threads from pulling it also lengthens their life. They should be dried by laying out on a flat surface. Never hang up knitted silk or wool garments.

Knitted woollen garments will regain their original elasticity and stiffness if you finish them off by putting them into a solution of a pint of hot water, a pint of thick, boiling-water starch and a teaspoonful of glue. Let the solution get cool, and when the garment is half dry dip it in, then lay it flat on a towel to re-dry.

TO CLEAN A MACKINTOSH SUCCESSFULLY

Mackintoshes are cleaned with cold water and soap solution. If your mac is very dirty, soak it overnight in a large tub with 2 ozs. of dissolved borax, which will loosen the dirt. Then you can scrub it with a soft brush. It should be hung up to dry on a hanger without squeezing the water out of it first, as you must be careful not to crease the rubber. A rubber mac cannot, of course, be ironed, so pull it and smooth it out with your hands as it gradually dries. Never use patent cleaners on mackintoshes as they may rot the rubber. If you have grease stains on a mackintosh, try rubbing Fuller's earth into them, leaving for some time, and then removing the absorbed grease gently with your finger-nails.

SHOPPING FOR MATERIALS

WHEN you go to buy material, know first what you intend to use it for. It is always a good plan to buy your paper pattern first, then to get a material to suit it. This also ensures that you get the right yardage. For instance, if you are going to make an afternoon frock with gathered drapery, you must buy a material that will hang softly. If you are making a tailored frock or blouse, get a fairly stiff fabric that will tailor into pleats and tucks without a lot of trouble.

Are you a bargain hunter? If you are, do watch yourself when you set off for the sales. "Such a bargain, my dear," is no bargain at all if it is the wrong width for the garment you need, or a colour that does not match your existing clothes. Before you start out, make a list of garments in your wardrobe that need replacing or altering, and the types and yardage of fabrics you need for replacement and alteration.

WHAT YOU CAN DO WITH THESE LENGTHS

You can make a blouse from two yards of 36-inch material, provided you do not choose a plaid or a pattern that has an " up and down " to it and needs piecing. From a yard of material you can make a pair of bias-cut French knickers. From 1½ yards you can make a vest; from 2½ yards a vest and knicker set or a petticoat. A brassière for the average figure takes ¾ yard. Three-quarters of a yard will make a three-cornered scarf to tie round your head, tuck into your neck, or drape round the throat of a tired black dress. Half-a-yard will make collars and cuffs, a couple of new pockets, a sash or belt. Don't buy remnants indiscriminately. See you have a use for them, and buy only colours that match your existing colour scheme.

TO WED MATERIAL TO STYLE

When buying material for a frock or coat, have a regard for the pattern in relation to the fabric. Checks, plaids, stripes or materials with a knobbly surface look silly if they are gathered, draped or cut in too wide flares. They need tailored styles. Any pattern with intricate and beautiful detail, such as piped seams or pockets, unusual neck-lines, hip-lines, tucks or hand-run gathers at the waist, should be made up in a plain material. It loses its point if the detail is submerged in a print.

Printed and flowered fabrics should be made up in simple styles, as the frock is relying for effect on the material itself and not on the detail of the sewing. The same thing applies to lingerie. If you like your lingerie with lace or embroidery on it, choose a plain material with a certain amount of " body " to it. Ruffles and gathers look better on printed voiles, tiny-flowered silks and chiffon.

SIMPLE TESTS FOR QUALITY

There are ways of judging before you buy them whether or not materials will wear well. Pure silk wears almost for ever. Take a sample home and burn it. If it burns clean away, leaving a very fine ash, then it is pure silk ; if it is inclined to smoulder and leaves a thickish dark ash, it is either weighted or sized. You can tell if silk is sized while you are still in the shop by wetting your finger and pressing it on the silk. If it makes your finger sticky it's sized. In war-time a lot of silks are bound to be weighted, and although they then have less elasticity it can't be helped. Sized silks, however, should be avoided if possible, as the sizing will come out when they're laundered and leave them flabby and thin.

When buying woollens choose those that are closely woven, as you'll get better wear out of them. Crumple a woollen material up in your hand to see if it creases badly. Unless the creases spring out in a minute or two it's not a wise buy. This applies also to buying linen.

Cotton can be tested for its wearing qualities by picking a piece up in the hand and rubbing the two surfaces together. If the texture becomes roughened it won't wear clean, and when in constant use will quickly develop a rough surface.

THE VALUE OF A TRADE-MARK

Whenever you can, choose " branded " fabrics, as these usually carry some kind of guarantee by the makers, and if they should accidentally wear badly, or you should be unlucky enough to get hold of an imperfect length, the manufacturers can be approached direct in the matter, and will sometimes replace the length of fabric for you. On the same principle it is wise to go to a store which has a reputation for selling only materials that are value for money.

HOW THE WIDTHS RUN

Different types of materials are made up in different widths. Silks, fine wools and cottons are usually 36 inches wide. Heavy woollens, tweeds, and fur fabrics are from 52 inches to 54 inches wide, shantung and tussore from 27 to 33 inches wide. Corduroy and velveteen are from 24 to 27 inches wide.

The width of the material you buy determines the yardage

for your garment. You'll need roughly 4 to 4½ yards of 36-inch material for a frock for a stock-size figure (36-inch bust). A short-sleeved blouse takes about 2 yards, a skirt 2½ yards.

If you buy a 54-inch width you can make a slightly flared skirt from a yard of material, while a frock takes only 2½ yards. Wider materials naturally cost more per yard than narrower ones, but as less material is needed they are not an extravagance. Also, there is less waste in cutting out on a wide fabric.

LOVELY CLOTHES FROM FURNISHING FABRICS

For a dressing-gown, house-coat, or evening frock consider buying a furnishing fabric. Some of the artificial silk damasks and brocades in the furnishing department can be turned into lovely clothes. They have the advantage of being rather heavier than dress materials and will therefore wear better and are warmer. Also, they can be bought in double widths, which means anything from 54 to 70 inches wide. For instance, a house-coat for the average figure, in a 36-inch fabric, will take seven yards of material; in a 54-inch material it takes only five.

If you pay 3/11 a yard for your material (which is approximately the price that both a printed artificial silk dress fabric and an artificial silk furnishing damask would cost), you save eight shillings by buying the damask. And you get a better-wearing and more luxurious-looking garment.

SAVING ON CLOTHES AT THE LINENS COUNTER

The household linen department of a big store is another happy hunting-ground for fabrics that may be turned into clothes. I have seen charming candy-stripe cottons at 6d. a yard, intended for kitchen curtains, made up into summer frocks for an eight-year-old girl. The same type of fabric and design would have cost more than double in the dress material section. Light-weight furnishing hessian in lovely clear colours at 1/6 a yard can be made into children's dungarees, or into a loose lumber-jacket for yourself. Pastel-coloured Turkish roller-towelling at 1/6 a yard, 24 or 27 inches wide, will make useful summer dressing-gowns for small children. They can be rubbed out in the weekly wash and need no ironing.

A SNAG IN BUYING REMNANTS

One last word about remnants. Don't take the widths for granted when you buy them. Have them measured. Often odd pieces of really beautiful materials find their way to the remnant counter, and are marked at little cost because they are too narrow a width to do much with. This applies particularly to brocades, taffeta, velveteen and hand-printed silks.

TOOLS YOU CANNOT DO WITHOUT

LEARN to sew for yourself and save money. Professional-looking dressmaking is not difficult to do once you know a few fundamental rules, and if you start off by buying yourself good equipment.

The amateur dressmaker usually begins badly by not bothering about the right tools. Quite a number of women will try to cut out their lingerie with a pair of nail-scissors, and then wonder why it doesn't fit.

GOOD SCISSORS ARE ESSENTIAL

Get yourself a good pair of scissors to start with. Steel cutting-out scissors with double-sided handles (so that they don't cut into the joint of your thumb when you're using them) cost about 3/11 a pair. Larger ones for tailoring jobs on heavy materials cost from 7/- to 10/- a pair. Spending money on good scissors is a long-sighted economy, as you will then get cleanly-cut lines and your garment will be well fitting. The scissors should always be kept sharp, of course, and this can be done at home by opening the blades against the neck of a strong glass bottle, and then closing them slowly as if trying to cut the neck off the bottle. Do this about twenty times, and you'll get a lovely edge on your scissors.

Other necessary equipment is steel pins (about 1/- a box), as these won't rust or mark your fabric, a tape measure made of good strong material so that it doesn't stretch and become inaccurate, tailor's chalk for marking (this costs only a few pence, saves tacking, and brushes off the material easily), and a steel thimble. See that the indentations on the thimble are deep enough to hold your needle firmly, but not so deep that your needle will catch in them if you are doing a quick job of work like large tacking stitches. If you cannot get a steel thimble, choose a bone one in preference to one of a softer metal. After a time, the needle often goes right through these thin metal thimbles.

OTHER AIDS TO DRESSMAKING

These are all the things that are absolutely necessary. Additional helps which cost only a few shillings all told, but which may be difficult to get in war-time, are a tracing-wheel and a yard-stick. A tracing-wheel is a little free-wheel instrument which you can run around the edges of a paper pattern laid on your material so that it makes a slight indentation on the fabric, and thus marks an even line for cutting. The thin edge of a piece of tailor's chalk can be used equally well to mark such a line. A yard-stick is used mainly to measure the length of a skirt-hem from the ground so that it is turned up evenly all round. A long ruler would do as well.

Another great aid and time-saver in the home dressmaker's equipment is a pair of pinking shears to neaten inside seam edges. These are like scissors, but have serrated edges so that they cut out the edges of material into little triangles. They save the labour of doing this with small scissors when the garment is finished, and on thick fabrics they save overcasting seam edges. At the price of about a guinea, however, they may seem rather more than you can afford, and, of course, it is possible to manage without them.

SAVING TIME AND TEMPER WITH NEEDLES

Needles and thread should be of the best quality. Needles are bought by sizes, the larger the number the smaller the needle. For fine lingerie use a No. 10 needle, for ordinary work a No. 7 or 8. Many people will buy packets of assorted needles from 3-8, but one packet of assorted needles can often be a nuisance, as you are apt to lose or break the needle you want to use just when the shops are shut. It is better to get three packets—one of No. 10 for fine sewing and finishing, one of No. 7 or 8 for ordinary sewing, and a packet of No. 3 or 4 for tacking and overcasting.

Once the point of your needle becomes blunt stop using it. It will tear your fabric and your nerves. If it becomes rough or rusty and doesn't slip easily through your work, draw it along a piece of fine emery paper. You can buy emery paper from any local ironmonger's shop for a penny a sheet.

Sewing-machine needles are supplied with the machine, and should be changed according to the fabric you are working on. Use thick needles for thick fabrics and *vice versa*. Puckering and uneven stitches in machined seams are often due to the fact that the wrong thickness of needle is being used.

BUY THREADS TO SUIT YOUR MATERIALS

When you buy cottons, always buy them at the same time as you buy your fabric, so that you get a perfect match. Use pure silk for your work, as it has more elasticity than cottons or silk substitutes and will not break when you're using it, or split later when the garment is in wear. It costs much more—about

7d. a reel—but is worth it in general wear and tear. Cotton garments should be sewn with cotton.

For tacking, buy proper spools of tacking thread which are specially made for the purpose and will not mark your material. Also, this thread does not tie itself into aggravating knots when you're busy with a particularly long seam. Machine cottons are of two types: a six-ply quality for the top spool, and a rather finer thread for the bobbin.

Keeping cotton reels in order is not easy, but I have found a solution which I think a good one. Thread the spools on to a thick, long knitting needle, and put a small cork on to the pointed end to prevent them slipping off. If you then remember always to slip the loose end of the thread back into its niche on the reel, you're almost bound to keep them tidy, and, of course, you can pull your thread off its reel without taking it off the knitting needle.

EQUIPMENT FOR PRESSING

Pressing is an important part of good dressmaking, and for proper pressing you need a fairly heavy iron, a skirt board and a sleeve board. Once you've got them, keep them clean.

A skirt board can be bought for about 9/11, and a sleeve board for about 5/11. When they are not in use they should be covered with a piece of old sheeting so that they don't get dusty. Also, when you are pressing keep an odd piece of material handy to try your iron on in case it is dirty or too hot. This saves the board from stains. A sleeve iron, with a special point for getting in between gathers, is a great help, and you should also have a sleeve pad and a shoulder pressing pad. These can be made of muslin and stuffed tightly with cotton rags.

TO MAKE THE MOST OF A SEWING-MACHINE

If you have a sewing-machine take good care of it. You can't expect it to work properly for you unless you do. Also get your money's worth by learning how to use it. A sewing-machine will do many time-saving tricks for you such as hemming, binding, tucking and quilting, but many women fight shy of learning to use the gadgets that do these things.

One of the most common causes of a badly-running machine is dust. Dust your machine before and after you use it, and never put it away without the cover on. If it does not run smoothly, oil it, but use only the most superior machine oil bought direct from the makers of the machine. One drop of oil is enough. If you use more you will clog the mechanism. See that bobbin case and spring are free from fluff. These parts can be kept clean with a large, soft-bristled paint brush.

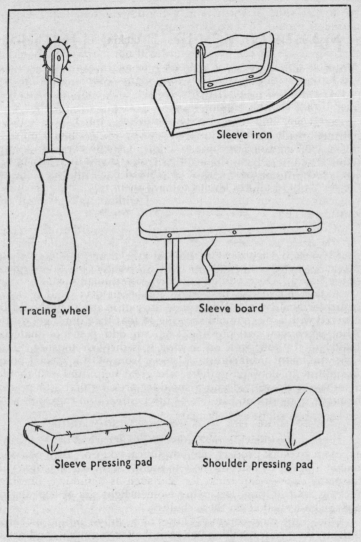

Sleeve iron

Tracing wheel

Sleeve board

Sleeve pressing pad

Shoulder pressing pad

1. EQUIPMENT TO ENSURE A TRIM FINISH.

Use fine needles and thread on fine fabrics, a thick needle and thread on heavier ones. If the thread snaps, the material puckers or the stitches loop, your tension is wrong. Look at the booklet of directions and adjust the tension accordingly.

MAKING YOUR OWN UNDIES

YOUR friends may have told you, when there were so many ready-made, well-cut and prettily-decorated undies on the market at a low price, that it was not worth while to make your own. This is a short-sighted policy, for while in many cases the material you buy may cost you nearly as much as a finished garment ready-made, and more coupons, you get better material for the price, and home-made undies last three times as long. Now that prices have risen and it is not always possible.to buy your favourite make or shade of lingerie, you will find it doubly worth while to make undies at home.

THE LINGERIE YOU NEED

Gone are the days when any of us have either the money or the space to possess six of everything in our undies drawer. But you should try to have three of everything, one set on your back, one in the wash, and one clean and ready for any emergency that may crop up. What you need is three brassières, three nightdresses (or three pairs of pyjamas), three pairs of cami-knickers (or vest and knicker sets) and three slips. These, made up in the best materials you can afford, carefully washed and regularly mended, should last from 2½ to 3 years before they need replacing. Buy them now a little better than you usually do, and they will need fewer replacements and therefore less expenditure of coupons.

Corsets should be bought two pairs at a time, and three if you can find the money. Regular laundering of corsets helps to keep their shape and elasticity.

UNDIES TO SUIT ALL TYPES OF FROCKS

The style and cut of your undies depend on your personal taste, and on the style of the garments under which they are to be worn.

Tailored underclothes made with tucks, pleats and simple embroidery, such as a monogram, are best made up in crêpe-de-chine, satin, rayon, or spun silk, or in fine cambric or cotton. The more fussy type of undies with lace trimmings, ruffles and frills look better in fine voiles, chiffon or muslin. In winter some women will prefer to wear knitted underwear, but if you don't care for wool there are plenty of winceys and fine flannels made in plain pastel colours, or sprigged with tiny flower patterns on a pastel ground.

Underclothes to be worn under tailored frocks and suits

should be well fitting and cut on the straight, so that the weave of every garment you are wearing falls in the same direction. Never wear a shiny-surfaced fabric such as satin under a tailored skirt, for the skirt will slip on the material. A heavy rayon, artificial taffeta, or rough-surfaced spun silk is a far better choice to wear under tailored clothes.

Chiffons or voiles are worn under silk and fine wool dresses. The thinner your dress, the thinner should be the underclothes you wear with it, to help the hang and cut of the dress. Thick materials should be worn over undies made up in materials with a certain amount of " body " to them.

HOW TO MAKE LINGERIE LAST

Materials that wash well and can be ironed with a fairly hot iron are satin, crêpe-de-chine, chiffon, muslin and crêpe suzette. All artificial silks should be washed in water that is only warm, and ironed with a very cool iron. Rayon has excellent washing and wearing qualities, but care should be taken not to stretch the garment when washing it, and to pull it out into shape gently before it is hung up to dry.

Lock-knit materials are best not made up at home. They are apt to ladder easily, and need such careful piecing together so that the threads do not pull in opposite directions, that the home dressmaker is wise not to attempt to make them up herself.

Flared skirts should always have bias-cut petticoats beneath them. A word about ironing bias-cut undies. Always iron them on the way of the weave, a small piece at a time. Don't make long up and down strokes of the iron as you would on a piece of straight material. Rather press them gently, putting the iron down and lifting it off rapidly. This keeps their shape, and the hems of bias-cut petticoats will not drop.

MAKE YOUR OWN PAPER PATTERNS

THERE are many excellent undies patterns on the market for all shapes and styles of garments but, owing to the paper shortage, it will become increasingly difficult as the war goes on to obtain paper patterns of any description. It is therefore as well to know how to make your own paper patterns.

This is largely a matter of taking careful and correct measurements. Once you have an accurate basic pattern for your own figure many garments may be cut from it.

TO MEASURE FOR LINGERIE

Start off by measuring your natural waist-line. Draw the tape-measure in fairly tightly. Write the measurements down on a piece of paper as you go along. Measure your bust right round with the tape-measure held slackly, then measure across your chest from arm-hole to arm-hole and about three inches below the neck-line.

Measure the length of line from your throat to your natural waist-line, and at the back from the nape of your neck to the waist-line. The side measurements are taken from well up in the arm-pit to the waist. Now measure the wide part of the shoulder-blades right across the back and the depth of arm-hole.

To measure a sleeve, stand with your arm bent so that you allow yourself elbow-room, and measure from the top of the outer arm to the wrist.

Skirt measurements are taken from the waist-line down to the hem-line at the front, back, and sides. Hip measurements are taken with a slack inch-tape about nine inches below the natural waist-line.

Having got your size " taped," you are now ready to draft a basic paper pattern for yourself which will not only stand you in good stead when you can no longer buy paper patterns, but will prove of enormous help if you find you have to adjust bought patterns. Remember that all turnings are allowed for in these home-made patterns.

A BODICE PATTERN WITH MANY PURPOSES

To make a bodice pattern that you can use for a petticoat, a nightdress, or a simple frock, cut an oblong piece of paper about 10 inches wide by 18 inches deep for the back. To cut the neck, measure about half-an-inch down from the top left-hand corner, then cut the paper away in a slight curve about 3 inches long. The shoulder slant is cut by measuring 6½ inches along from the top right-hand corner, and 2½ inches down. On this point cut upwards to meet the end of the neck-line. From the far point of the shoulder slant, measure the depth of the arm-hole, then from the left-hand side of the paper measure across a quarter of your bust measurement. Cut the arm-hole curve from this point. The length of the back of the bodice is your measurement from the nape of the neck to the waist-line.

To shape the waist, draw a straight line down from the bottom edge of the arm-hole to the waist. Then measure a couple of inches in at the waist-line, and cut up from this to the bottom point of the arm-hole in a gradual slant. To further tighten the waist, mark a dart 3 inches along from the centre of the back, about 3 inches long and half-an-inch wide. You now have your back bodice pattern.

The front half of the pattern is made out of a larger oblong of paper, this time 12 inches wide by 19 inches deep. Also, the cutting is started from the right-hand side of the paper. Measure 3 inches along from the right, 4 inches down, and cut the neck curve. From the right-hand corner again, measure along 9 inches and down 3 inches. From this point up to the top of the neck makes the shoulder slant.

The arm-hole for the front bodice has to be slightly larger than for the back, as there is the fullness of the bust to consider. Add another inch to the back arm-hole measurement (or if you are a 38-inch or 40-inch bust, another 2 inches), and mark this point from the top right-hand corner. Then measure across a quarter of your bust-size, plus a couple of inches, and cut the arm-hole in a full curve from this point to the top edge of the shoulder. The waist is shaped in the same way as for the back bodice pattern.

The shoulder-lines and waist-lines will need to be adjusted to a perfect fit by darts. Generally speaking, the dart on the shoulder is best placed about 4 to 5 inches from the neck-line, and made about 7 inches long and about 1½ inches wide. The dart at the waist-line is marked in the same way as for the back bodice pattern.

This gives you a basic pattern for a vest, blouse or jacket, and the top of a petticoat, nightdress or frock.

A SIMPLE VEST PATTERN

To cut a simple vest according to this basic pattern you need the oblong of paper 30 inches deep by 12 inches wide. To make the underarm, measure in 7 inches from the top right-hand corner, 3 inches down, and cut away in a very slightly-sloped curve. From the top left-hand corner measure in 3 inches, and down 3½ inches, then cut down sharply to this point. This gives you a brassière-top. Make a dart right down the centre of the 2 inches of material left at the top, for bust fullness and fitting. Make a second dart 4 inches long and 2 inches wide, 2 inches below the underarm curve. The vest is shaped by cutting along an inward curve measuring 10 inches across at the waist-line, and gradually out again to the full 12-inch width as you reach the bottom.

The back is even simpler, for there is no shaping to be done at the top. Just measure 9 inches straight across at the top of the 12-inch wide paper, and then gradually cut down in an inward sloping curve the whole 30-inch length of the material, graduating your cutting so that the full 12 inches across is reached again at the bottom. Join up the two side-seams, hem the top and bottom, sew on 14-inch long shoulder-straps and you've made your vest in an evening. It takes a yard-and-a-half of material.

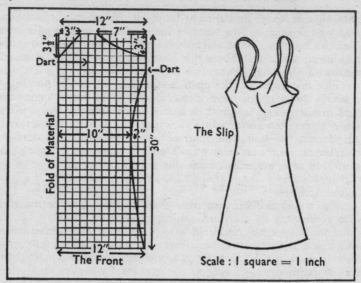

2. *To make a pattern for a well-fitting slip, cut out the front from a rectangle of paper 30″ by 12″ as shown. The back is cut from the same amount of material but the top requires no shaping.*

An excellently fitting slip can be cut from this same pattern, making it from 42 inches to 44 inches long, and allowing a width of 18 inches round the bottom. Two-and-a-half yards of 36-inch wide material will make the slip.

A SLIP FOR A FLARED SKIRT

If you prefer your petticoats more shaped, use the basic bodice pattern that has already been described and attach a skirt at the waist-line. This is the way to cut out a pattern for a slightly flared skirt ; the same pattern is used for the front and back. Cut an oblong of paper 30 inches long and 36 inches wide. From the top left-hand corner measure across 18 inches, then from the same corner measure down 2 inches. From this point cut up in a gentle curve to the point measured 18 inches along the top. Make sure that the line you cut is not more than 2 inches from the top of the paper when you get to the centre of the skirt, i.e., 9 inches from where you start cutting.

Measure down 8 inches from the waist-line, and mark in the hip-line curve, which should exactly follow the line of the waist curve, and measure from 23 inches to 24 inches across, according to the relative width of your own waist and hips. In most people the hips are larger in proportion to the waist than they should be. The ruling is to mark this point the width of *half* your all-round hip measurements, plus a couple of inches. Cut the bottom of the skirt to follow the curve of waist- and hip-lines, making it about 36 inches across. Then, from the bottom right-hand corner of the skirt, cut up in a slanting straight line to meet the top right-hand point of the waist-line.

This skirt makes a perfectly good waist-length petticoat, and in these days of strict economy many women will wish to wear their petticoats from the waist, for they then take only 1¾ yards of 36-inch wide material. Waist-length petticoats are suitable to wear under any frock except one made of very fine materials such as chiffon, cotton voile or muslin.

FRENCH KNICKERS FROM A YARD OF MATERIAL

Bias-cut French knickers can be made from a yard of material. This is the way to cut your own pattern for them.

Take a piece of paper 36 inches wide and 18 inches deep. Mark in 8 inches from either side at the top. Mark up 3½ inches from either side at the bottom. On this point cut a straight line inwards on each side at the bottom 1½ inches long, then cut up each side in an inward curve to meet the points at the top which you have already marked. It is as simple as this to make a pattern for French knickers, and these measurements fit the average figure. The same pattern is used for back and front.

The seams in this pattern are made in the centre and not at the sides of the garment, and the gusset is formed by the little side pieces that are cut in one with the main pattern. To cut out the knickers in fabric, the yard of material is laid out flat, and the pattern laid crosswise on the material *twice*. From the pieces of material left over at the sides, cut two strips on the straight of the material 1½ inches deep and 13 inches long. These pieces form the narrow waist-band for the top of the knickers.

A PATTERN FROM AN OLD PAIR OF KNICKERS

To make a pattern for a pair of directoire knickers at home, it is simplest to cut this from an old pair, as the making of this type of pattern from written directions is not easy. Undo the centre-seams and gusset-seams of an old pair of knickers. It is not necessary to unpick the side-seams, as the pattern is cut for the two portions, one for each leg. Spread the two separate legs out flat and cut from them. To make the garment up, the short inside-seam of each leg section should be joined, and then the two halves joined together by the centre-edges, from the front waist-line, right round and up again to the back waist-line.

The waist and the bottoms of the legs are then turned under and threaded with elastic. The average measurements for a pair of directoire knickers are 26 inches side length from the waist to the ground when kneeling, and the hip measurement (taken 8 inches below the natural waist-line) 40 inches round.

A BRASSIÈRE OR PETTICOAT TOP

Brassières should always be made of fairly stiff material, such as silk piqué, taffeta or rayon with a good " body." If you are making them from pieces of fabric you have bought to make a set of lingerie, such as chiffon, fine crêpe-de-chine, or thin satin, back them with net, and insert little triangles of wide elastic (which can be bought by the yard) along the lower edges of the brassière where they fit beneath the breast. This strengthens the material and gives added support.

A paper pattern for a brassière is easiest of all to make. Cut two pieces of material 12 inches square. See that you cut an exact square. If you have a 38-inch or 40-inch bust, the squares will have to be 14 inches each side. Fold the two squares in half, so that you have two triangles of double material. Lay one triangle over the other about 7 inches along the base, and machine down in a small triangle. Turn under all the edges in a narrow hem, and on the right-hand triangle attach a strip of material about 2 inches wide to form a band across the back. Turn in the bottom left-hand edge of the left-hand triangle about 1½ inches and sew on eyes to fasten into the hooks, which must be set on the end of the strip joined to the right-hand triangle. Two darts, 2 inches long and 1 inch wide, at the centre base of each triangle will make the brassière fit snugly beneath the breast.

This brassière also makes an excellent top for an evening slip to wear with an evening frock that is cut low at the back. The skirt for such a slip may be cut from the foundation pattern already described, and the top of the skirt eased on to the bottom edge of the brassière. With such a snug-fitting brassière top it is unnecessary to wear a brassière as well as the petticoat, so that if your evening frock is sheath-like you need not make yourself look bulky with underwear.

TO MAKE AND ATTACH SHOULDER-STRAPS

If you wish to make shoulder-straps of self-material to match the garment, follow the method you would use for making a simple belt. Cut a strip of material about ¾ inch wide and, folding it lengthwise, run the two raw edges together, and turn inside out as you go along. The seam when finished should be in the centre-back of the strap.

Lingerie straps should be sewn on to the garment on the wrong side at the bottom of the top hem, and caught with light stitches at the sides. To prevent them slipping off the shoulder, they are placed nearer together at the back of the garment than at the front. Allow about 10 inches between the straps at the front and 8 inches at the back.

FINE SEAMS FOR DELICATE LINGERIE

IF YOU have the time and the patience, do try to make your lingerie by hand. It looks better, and on delicate fabrics hand-made seams and hems last much longer than if they are made by machine ; also, they help the " hang " of the garment.

The great thing about putting lingerie together is to avoid any kind of clumsiness, and for this reason only the finest ways of seaming and finishing are used.

TO MAKE A SMALL, NEAT SEAM

Edges should be joined by French seaming, or by a seam and fell. To make a French seam, run the raw edges together on the *right* side of the material with tiny running stitches done with a fine needle. Keep as close to the edge as you can without the material fraying, and every sixth stitch make a

Right side

Wrong side

3. HOW TO MAKE A FRENCH SEAM.

back-stitch to strengthen the seam. Then turn the garment inside out on to the wrong side, and press the tiny seam between the edges of the material with your thumb and finger-nail to flatten it. Seam down again with the same running-stitches on the wrong side, encasing the seam already made. The advantage of this method of seaming lingerie is that you keep your seam edges very small.

A seam and fell is done on the wrong side of the garment. The front raw edge is placed a little lower than the back one, and seamed down flat with small running stitches. Then the top edge is turned over and hemmed down flat over the running stitches. Open the garment out as flat as possible to avoid catching up the back of the material when you are hemming.

TO TRIM LINGERIE

IN WAR-TIME you will probably have neither the time nor the inclination to apply elaborate lace and embroidery trimmings to lingerie. If you have any lace by you which you care to use for this purpose, you may like to apply it as an edging to slips and knickers, but the easiest and most practical trimming is bias binding. You can achieve some very attractive finishes by using binding in colours that contrast with the garment itself.

It is easier to buy binding than to cut binding strips from your material. Binding costs only a few pence a yard ; it is cut on the cross and the edges are already turned under for you. Choose turquoise blue binding on peach-coloured undies or, if you are making up a printed floral material, use binding that picks up the predominant colour in the pattern. A plain trimming of this sort looks well with an embroidered monogram at the top in the same colour as the binding.

FROCKS, BLOUSES AND SKIRTS

MAKING your own clothes can be a very satisfying personal adventure. Not only do you get your clothes for one-third of what they would cost you ready-made, but each garment you turn out is exclusive. You will never meet anyone else in the frock you make yourself. Plenty of other women may buy the same pattern, but it is a million to one against another woman making it up in the same material, or with the same finishing touches that you yourself may use.

If you sew for yourself, you'll have more money to spend on shoes, hats, belts and gloves. If you have a family and you sew for them all, then there's more money to spend on food, or to put into National Savings.

I have already talked about the materials that are used for different types of frocks, so go and get your material, take a good look at the illustration on the front of the pattern envelope, and make up your mind that your frock is going to look just as attractive on you as it does on the model in the drawing.

GETTING READY TO CUT OUT

Now get down to it. I say " get down to it " advisedly, for the best place to do your cutting out is on the floor. Every piece of the pattern should be pinned on the material before you start cutting, and few of us have tables large enough for this. So cover the floor with clean newspaper, and cut your material out on this. This method has another advantage over a polished table—the material doesn't slip about while you're cutting.

Don't, however, start either pinning or cutting until you are sure you know what the various pieces of the pattern mean, and that they are going to fit you.

In many patterns alternative versions of the garment are given. Go through each piece, therefore, and if there are any you do not need for the style you are going to make, put these away for the moment so that they don't confuse you when you start pinning the pattern on to the material.

TO ALTER A PATTERN TO FIT YOU

Now measure the pattern with an inch-tape and compare these measurements with your own.[1] You may find little discrepancies here and there, and these must be put right before you begin to cut. The golden rule in altering patterns is *never to alter the position of the waist-line.* If you do, you'll throw the hang of the skirt and the fit of the arm-hole out of gear.

[1] See p. 21.

If you are a short person and the pattern is too long, fold it over a couple of inches below the arm-hole, again at the hip-line, and shorten the hem. The amount you fold it over depends on the amount it has to be shortened, of course, but you can find this out only by comparing with your own measurements and making the depth of the folds accordingly. If the pattern is much too long, remember it is essential to distribute the reductions in this way. If you try to shorten the pattern entirely at the hem, you will make the bottom of the skirt too narrow. If you are tall, cut the pattern straight across a couple of inches below the arm-hole, and cut it across at the hip-line, then paste these cut pieces of pattern on to a large piece of paper as far apart as is necessary to give you the additional length you need. The hem can also be lengthened, but not enough to spoil the style by altering the slope of the side-seams.

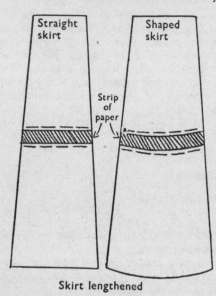

Skirt lengthened

4. To Adjust Skirt Patterns.

If sleeves are too long, the pattern should have a tuck taken in it just above and below where the elbow comes. If they are too short, the pattern should be cut straight across in the same places and the three pieces adjusted on another piece of paper until the right length is found, and then pasted down. A sleeve that is too narrow should have a piece of paper inserted lengthwise to make it the required width. A sleeve that is too wide should have a tuck taken down the middle. Whatever alterations you make to your sleeve pattern, however, you must, of course, be careful to preserve its shape. A lengthwise insertion of paper must be cut at the top to follow the shoulder curve.

Never alter the depth of the arm-hole on the pattern. Cut it out according to the measurements given (if you are thin or small cut it ½ inch from the edge of the pattern instead of right up close), then it can be adjusted when the side-seams are sewn up. To adjust arm-holes and neck-lines make a series of small

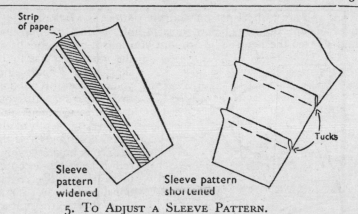

5. To Adjust a Sleeve Pattern.

slashes in towards the body of the garment until the fit is eased, then mark it round with tailor's chalk, and get somebody to cut it carefully while the garment is on you. It is always wiser to cut neck-lines and arm-holes rather smaller than instructed on the pattern if you are not sure. You can always cut material away, but once cut you can't put it back.

Sloping shoulders, very square shoulders and too big hip-lines are best dealt with when the garment is being tacked, as this is a case of altering seam-lines. In the case of shoulder-seams it affects the arm-hole, which may have to be cut a little deeper at the underarm to prevent it dragging. So don't cut your pattern about to remedy these faults.

Having got your pattern ready, iron out the creases in the material and lay it flat on the floor. Try, if you can, to be alone when you're cutting out, as you do need to know exactly what each piece is for. If you start talking to someone in the room, you won't keep your mind on it and the usual tragedy of cutting two sleeves for one arm will happen, for you'll forget to turn the pattern over for the second sleeve.

PINNING THE PATTERN ON THE MATERIAL

Look at the diagram given with the pattern and place the pieces accordingly. The selvedges of the material should face you. If you are working on velvet or on a patterned material, see that all the pieces lie in the same direction. Don't think you can get more out of your material by " just fitting this little bit in at the corner." Patterns are designed by experts, who know exactly what is to be got out of certain yardages, and the diagrams are worked out to get the most from the yardage given. If you start fitting in little bits, something will go wrong with your

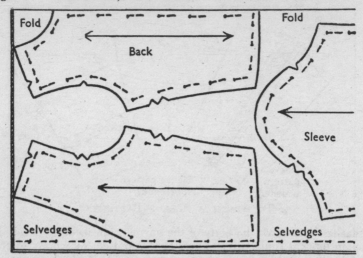

6. *When cutting out, have the selvedges of the material towards you. Pin the pattern every 2 inches and about ½ inch from the edge. The arrows show the direction of the straight thread of the material.*

finished garment, such as a dragging sleeve, because you've done some " fitting in " on the wrong way of the material—or even a bit of the design on the fabric will turn out to be upside down !

Pin the pattern to the material about half-an-inch on the inside edge all the way along, and at intervals of a couple of inches. It may seem a lot of pinning, but it saves the material from pulling or slipping and makes all the difference to the hang of the finished garment.

DIRECTIONS IT IS VITAL TO FOLLOW

When you start cutting, use the middle of the blades of your scissors and cut with long, even strokes. Never cut the notches which may be marked in the pattern. These must be marked with tailor's chalk or a tacking thread. When you have cut out all the pieces, do not unpin the pattern. Leave it attached to the material until you have marked in all notches, darts and tucks. Each piece of the garment should be laid flat on the table and have these directions marked in with either chalk or tacking thread. This is *not* a waste of time. Guessing at where seams join, guessing at where darts and tucks should be placed, leads to a lop-sided frock. Tailor's tacks are good for marking in the small perforations showing where darts should come. They are made by taking a couple of loop-stitches where the

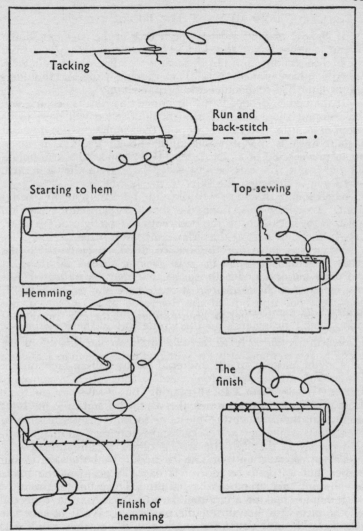

Tacking

Run and
back-stitch

Starting to hem

Top-sewing

Hemming

The
finish

Finish of
hemming

7. *If you are new to dressmaking, first practise these basic stitches on spare material until you can do them neatly.*

perforations come, through the pattern and the material (both thicknesses if your material is double), then clipping the threads so that little tufts are left on each side. Notches are more easily marked with chalk.

HOW TO MAKE THE BODICE FIT

If you are making a dress, the bodice of the garment should be put together before the skirt. Unpin the paper pattern from the bodice sections, and pin the seams together where indicated. When you have pinned, tack. Tack the side-seams and shoulder-seams of the bodice together and then try it on.

If the bodice droops badly at either side, this is because you have sloping shoulders, and the shoulder-seams will have to be taken up a little. Do this by sloping the shoulder-seams down at a slant towards the arm-hole until enough material is taken up to prevent the drooping sides. It will make the arm-hole a bit tight, but this can be cut away later from the underarm when you've attached the skirt to the bodice.

High square shoulders will drag the bodice up at the centre-front. To adjust this, slope the shoulder-seams up a fraction towards the neck-line. If the bodice itself is too tight or too loose, take in more, or less, at the side-seams, until it fits.

When you have got the bodice fitted, machine-stitch the pieces together and put in with tacking thread all darts at the neck-line and under the arms that may be indicated. As you machine each seam press it out flat on the wrong side. If you keep your iron hot all the time, and press as you go, not only do you get a better-looking garment at the end, but also it is encouraging to you, for odd wrinkles and creases and dragging seams will frequently lie as flat as a table top once the seams are pressed. It is tremendously encouraging to be able to look at each section as you do it and say, " That bit fits beautifully."

JOINING THE SKIRT TO THE BODICE

You are now ready to tack the skirt. Pin and tack the side-seams first, then put in any pleats or tucks. It is permissible to press pleats while they are tacked and before they are machined, as if you *do* get them in the wrong places tacking threads are easier to remove than machine-stitching. Tack the skirt to the bodice and try on once more. If the skirt drops at the back, or the front, take up more seam on the *skirt* waist at the top.

If you are making a circular skirt, and you have to " piece " in a triangle of material at either seam edge at the bottom, do snip away the selvedges of the odd piece. You may think you are saving yourself the trouble of neatening a raw edge by using the selvedge, and so you are, but as selvedges are non-elastic you may get a nasty pull on your garment.

SUCCESS WITH SLEEVES

The thought of putting sleeves into a garment is often a nightmare to the amateur. But as long as you have clearly marked the notches at the top of the sleeve, and round the armholes of the bodice, you cannot go far wrong.

First of all, tack up the sleeve-seams, and then, placing the underarm seam of the sleeve *exactly* over the underarm sleeve of the bodice, right side to right side, turn your garment inside out and proceed to pin the sleeve in all the way round the arm-hole. If it looks to you as though it isn't going to fit at the top, don't start cutting the material away to try to make it fit. That extra fullness is there for a purpose (to prevent the sleeve dragging at the shoulder-seam and cutting into your armpit), so take pains to ease it in. Usually this can be done by gathering the material up slightly with a gathering thread run fairly close to the raw edge of the top of the sleeve. Another way of doing it is to make three darts about 2 inches long, one dead in the centre of the top of the sleeve, and one each side of it.

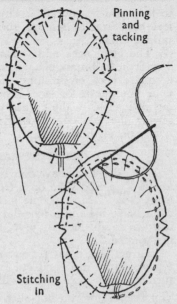

8. *Pin and tack sleeves to their garment, and try on before stitching them in position.*

When you have pinned the sleeve, tack it and try on the bodice with the set-in sleeves. If you find the inside seam is dragging at the elbow, that means you've set the back of the sleeve too much round to the front, and it must be untacked and moved backwards. If the material drags on the outside of the sleeve, then the front is too much round to the back, and it must be un-picked and brought forward. If it is baggy at the elbow, take up this extra fullness by making three small darts on the inside of the elbow-seam, and at right angles to it.

When you have got the sleeves correctly set, try the whole garment on again, inside out, to see that all of it fits you. Remember that a good fit doesn't mean a *tight* fit, but merely that all the lines should hang vertically from the waist, and that there is no drag at any of the cross-seams, such as at the underarms and the waist. Hip-lines are made smaller by taking in the side-seams, being careful to taper them off gradually into the skirt. A too full waist is given a more snug fit by a couple of darts at the back about 4 inches deep and 2 inches wide. Get a friend to help you fit yourself. Pin the alterations, and when they feel comfortable, remove the pins and mark them in with tailor's chalk.

The hem, neck and wrists should all be finished by hand. This is the hall-mark of a well-made garment. If you are binding a square neck or finishing the corner of the wrist-hem, mitre your binding as for lace. This means cutting a small triangle out of it close to the corner you are going to bind, and over-sewing the two edges together at the back. It will then fit neatly on to the corner.

THE SECRET OF MAKING A POINTED YOKE

I wonder if you have ever been bewildered and bad-tempered about a pointed yoke on a frock, or a skirt that has a pointed front piece ? Most people have at one time or another ; they can't make it lie in a nice flat point, and end up by machining it down in an uneven curve, hoping it will " look better when it's pressed."

To get this point professional-looking, turn it down at the top about an inch and cut it off, then fold under your seam turnings, and you'll find it will not only lie flat, but will also lie in a perfect point.

The top of the sleeves of your dress, if there is any gathered fullness, should be pressed carefully with the point of the iron so that you do not flatten any gathers. Press the seam open flat and then run the point of the iron up into the gathers from elbow to neck-line.

TO FACE A NECK OR OPENING

The V-neck, or back opening of a dress, is usually finished off by a facing. Facings are joined by the shoulder-seams. Tack the facing, right side of the material downwards, on to the right side of the garment. Tack right round the opening, then machine down, close to the edge. Press open the seams, then turn the facing in on to the wrong side, and press again flat on the wrong side. The raw edges of the facing should be neatly hemmed on a fine material, overcast on a rougher one. If it is a wide facing, put in one or two invisible stitches to hold it down to the main section of the garment.

COLLARS THAT WILL REALLY FIT

The making and fitting of collars can be a bane, and do need care and a certain amount of knowledge. First see that your neck-line fits you. If it is too small, enlarge it by means of small vertical slashes until it is easier, mark it with chalk, and cut away to fit. If it is too large, make it smaller by means of darts at the back—about three darts at the centre-back of the neck, 3 inches long and 1 inch wide should be enough. It is a good idea in these days to finish your neck-line completely as though it were going to be collarless, and then make detachable collars. This should always be done, of course, where you are going to use " lingerie touches," i.e. collars and cuffs in a light-coloured material, or of piqué, silk or linen.

Non-detachable collars, double or single, should be partially made up before they are sewn on to the garment. Be sure that your collar is the same size as your neck-line, and that both sides of the collar match. Lightly hem down the outside edges, taking great care not to bring your needle through on to the right side of the collar. The inside edge of the collar which is to be attached to the neck-line should be bound with a strip of bias or Prussian binding. Then fold your collar exactly in half, and mark on it with a pin where the centre-back comes. Attach the collar to the garment with pins at the centre-back, and both sides at the front. Tack, and then turn under the binding and sew it down.

TO ATTACH A DOUBLE COLLAR

A double collar should be machined down all round close to the edge, right sides together, except along the neck edge. Press open the seam, turn inside out, and press the whole collar flat. The under portion of the collar is then laid flat on the neck-line of the dress on the inside of the dress. Pin and tack smoothly, being careful to get the centre-back of the collar exactly on the centre-back point of the dress, and the two fronts perfectly level with the neck-line edge. Sew this down by hand (back-stitching frequently to make the seam firm). The front edge is then turned over and slip-stitched down to the seam. The inside seams should be pressed flat with a fairly hot iron over a damp cloth. I would advise you always to put on collars by hand, as there are several thicknesses of material involved, and any suggestion of clumsiness must be avoided.

A SIMPLE BELT

To make a flat belt of self-fabric, cut out a piece of material double the width you wish the belt to be. Then sew the raw edges together, right side to right side, with running-stitch, taking a back-stitch every other stitch to make it firm. Turn it inside out as you go along, a little piece at a time. Then press flat. If you need a stiffer belt, the fabric should be sewn over canvas or buckram. The material is turned in at the edges and then tacked down on to the buckram. When you have tacked it down, slip-stitch the edges together, so that the stitching does not show, and remove the tacking threads.

TO AVOID THAT " MISSING BUTTON "

If you are buying accessories for your dress, such as buttons and collars, see that you buy one more button than you need, so that when you lose one you can replace it. It is a great nuisance to have to buy a whole set of new buttons because you lose one. When buying ready-made collars, see that they are the same measurement as the neck-line of your dress.

PATTERNS FROM FAVOURITE CLOTHES

ONCE you have got your own measurements accurately " taped," it is not difficult to make your own paper patterns. Also, if you have a frock or a coat of which you have been very fond but which is now too old to wear, why not make a new garment on this pattern ? A dress you have liked, a short coat in which you have been admired, must have something about it that suits you, so copy it yourself in a length of new material. It is quite easy to make patterns from old garments, and you know before you start that the new garment is going to *fit* you.

TO CUT UP THE OLD GARMENT

If you have no further use for the garment, and can trust the steadiness of your hand and your patience, don't bother to unpick the seams. This is a waste of time. Cut the garment up as close as possible to the seam edge. If there are inserted pleats put in on a separate piece of material or separate godets, these should all be cut out. In the case of pleats, measure the width of the pleats across and the width they are from each other and jot these figures down on a piece of paper. When you have cut your garment up, iron out all the pieces carefully, taking care to *press* them (lifting the iron on and off rather than using long ironing strokes) so that you don't stretch them. They are then ready to be used as you would use a paper pattern, but remember that you have left no turnings, so leave ½-inch turnings all round as you cut.

To reckon what yardage you will need for a new garment cut on the pattern of an old one, measure the length of the garment (including depth of hem), then the width of it across the hip-line. Add together the length and hip measurements, then double them. Thus, if the length is 41 inches and the hips 36 inches, you require 36 inches + 41 inches × 2 = 154 inches. Add 18 inches for turnings, = 172 inches or 4 yards 28 inches.

TO TAKE A PATTERN WITHOUT UNPICKING

If there is still a certain amount of wear left in the garment you wish to use, and you cannot cut it up, pin sheets of paper to each portion of the garment, and trace the pattern carefully round the seam edges with a thick soft lead-pencil. A 4BB pencil has a soft lead that will not tear the paper. When you have traced the pattern round, cut it out before you unpin the paper.

Where you come into conflict with gathers, pleats and tucks on a garment of this type, the placing of these should be marked accurately on the pattern, and they should be measured across exactly, and three times the amount of material allowed for them as the space they take up. For instance, if you have 3 inches of tight gathers, or 3 inches of flat tucks on a shoulder-yoke, 9 inches extra of material should be allowed for these when you are cutting out from your new length.

If you have no old garments you wish to copy, and no money to spare for paper patterns, you can make your own patterns. Although they may take time in the beginning, they can be used for all sorts of garments, and as they are cut to fit your own measurements, they won't have to be adapted later.

DRESS PATTERNS YOU CAN MAKE FOR YOURSELF

THIS is the way to make a sleeve pattern to fit a foundation bodice pattern.[1] For this you need to take two accurate measurements of yourself ; the length of your arm, with the elbow bent, and the depth of your arm-pit, measuring up over the fat part of the arm at the top.

Cut out a piece of paper 26 inches long and 16 inches wide. Fold this across so that it is still 26 inches long, but now only 8 inches wide. Measure 5 inches down the fold of the paper, and from this point draw a straight line across, the length of half your top arm measurement, plus $1\frac{1}{2}$ inches. Turn the paper over and continue the line from the fold, on the other side, to the same length as the first line, so that the fold is in the centre of the line. This line is known as the crown line, and from it the rest of the sleeve pattern is built up.

The folded edge of the paper is now folded over again on to the farther point of the crown line. This makes a crease. Press it down well with your thumb nail so that the crease is clearly marked, and then open out flat again. You now have your original rectangle of 26 inches by 16 inches, with a centre crease and a crease down each side. From the top of the left-hand crease (at the top of the piece of paper) measure down 1 inch and mark the spot. From the top of the right-hand crease measure down $1\frac{1}{2}$ inches and mark it. The curve of the back of the sleeve is made by drawing an outward curve up from the

[1] See p. 22.

end of the crown line, through the 1-inch point already marked, and right up to the top of the centre crease of your rectangle of paper. The curve of the front of the sleeve is made by drawing a curve to graduate *inwards* from the end of the crown line to the point marked 1½ inches, and then a curve graduating *outwards* from this point up to the top of the centre crease. Cut round the lines you have drawn, and you have your basic pattern for a sleeve.

For a short sleeve, cut the pattern off just above the elbow. With this pattern, and the foundation pattern for a bodice,[1] you can make a simple long-sleeved blouse from 2 yards of material 36 inches wide.

A BLOUSE FROM YOUR OWN PATTERN

Place the back of the bodice pattern on a double width of material, with the centre-back on the fold. Two pieces are cut for the front, but the centre-front of the pattern is laid along the selvedges on a single width, so you must cut the front bodice pattern out twice. The sleeves should also be cut from single material.

To make up, join the side-seams and shoulder-seams, and inset the sleeves.[2] The left-hand raw edge at the front of the blouse is turned under and hemmed, while the right-hand front edge is given an overlapping facing, made of a straight strip of material 4 inches wide and the length of the front of the blouse. Join it to the raw edge, right side to right side, press out the seam, then fold the strip in half and turn it under to meet the seam you have just made. This makes a flap on which you can use either buttonholes or press-studs to do up the front of your blouse.

A DETACHABLE COLLAR PATTERN

The neck is finished as for a detachable collar. You can then make either a collar to fit it, or a ruffle for it. To make a collar, cut out a long rectangle of paper, 12 inches long by 6 inches deep. Measure up 3 inches from the bottom right-hand corner of the paper, and mark this point. Then measure along 9 inches from the top left-hand corner of the strip of paper, and draw a slanting line from here to meet the point you have already marked from the bottom right-hand corner. This gives you the edges of your collar. The top of the paper should then be cut in a gentle curve along to the 9-inch mark, and the bottom cut in a curve to match it, ending the bottom curve at the point marked 3 inches up. This pattern is for half a collar and should be cut on a double width of material.

[1] See page 22.   [2] See page 34.

A JUMPER FOR FORMAL OCCASIONS

To make a jumper for more formal wear the same pattern may be used, but for this you will need about 2½ yards of material, as the jumper has to come outside your skirt and greater length is needed, therefore, at the waist-line.

When cutting out the material to make the jumper, place the bodice section with the centre front on the fold of the material, so that there is no opening down the front of the jumper. The pattern also has to be cut longer. Mark a point 8 inches down from the waist-line on the centre fold. From this point measure straight across the width of *half* your hip measurements, plus half-an-inch for turnings. Cut on a slant from the end of the waist-line to this point.

When cutting out the neck-line of the front bodice, cut only a very shallow curve so that when made up it will hug your throat. To make it fit snugly round your hips, make two small darts at the hem about 4 inches long and 1 inch wide, each dart to come just over the hip-bone itself. Make another two darts at the back to correspond. The darts are best marked when you have tacked up the side-seams and tried the jumper on.

This jumper can be done up either at the back—a six-inch slit down the centre-back is enough—or else it can be fastened on the left shoulder. In the latter case leave this seam open, bind and press as though for a placket, and sew on small hooks and eyes or press-studs. It looks very well made up in heavy one-coloured pastel crêpe such as duck-egg blue or dusty pink.

A SKIRT TO GO WITH YOUR JUMPER

What about a neat skirt to go with that jumper? As the jumper is plain and has a fitted hip-line, it would be as well to keep the same straight line throughout the ensemble, and a skirt that is fairly tight over the hips and has an inverted pleat at the front for knee fullness would look delightful.

You'll need 2 yards of 36-inch material for the skirt for an average figure (waist 27, hips 38, length 30). Choose a closely-woven wool, navy or deep violet with a blue or pink jumper, or if you make your jumper up in a delicate green or warm yellow, nigger or black for the skirt.

This is how to make the pattern. Cut out a rectangle of paper 30 inches long by 17½ inches wide. From the bottom left-hand corner measure up 14 inches, and then measure in 3 inches at right angles to the edge of the paper. Draw a straight line up from the 3-inch mark to the top of the rectangle. At the top right-hand corner measure across 13 inches and mark this point. Then on the line where you have already cut in 3 inches, measure across 17 inches and mark this point. Draw a gently-sloping outward curve from the top right-hand corner where you've marked, through the second 17-inch point and down to the bottom of the rectangle. This gives you your front skirt pattern. The little piece that juts out is used to form the inverted pleat. When you've cut out the paper pattern, measure in 5 inches from the top left-hand corner, and mark a straight line 5 inches down for a dart.

To cut the back skirt pattern, cut another rectangle of paper 30 inches long by 11 inches wide. Measure 8 inches across the top from left to right, and mark this point. Measure down 16 inches along the left-hand side and across 10 inches, and mark this point. Then draw a line from the top right-hand 8-inch mark straight to the bottom of the rectangle, passing through the 10-inch mark as you go. This gives you the pattern for the back of the skirt. Mark in a dart 4 inches along from the top left-hand corner and 4 inches down from the top.

There has to be one more piece of pattern cut for the waist-band. This is simply a straight piece of paper 14 inches long and 2 inches wide, and fits round the top of the waist of the skirt, inside, like a facing.

Having got your pattern cut, the skirt can now be cut from the material. Iron out the material first to remove any creases, then fold it double. Place the front skirt pattern at the top of the material with the jutting-out piece lying against the fold. Pin it on to the material all round at the edge at 2-inch intervals. The back pattern is placed beneath it with the straight edge against the fold to avoid a seam down the centre-back. *Remember when you are cutting out this skirt to leave ¼ inch all round for turnings.*

TO MAKE UP THE SKIRT

Tack together the side-seams, and the seam at the centre-front of the skirt as far as the pleat. An opening should be left about 6 inches down the left-hand side of the skirt for the placket. Tack in the four darts and fit the skirt on, wrong side out. Adjust to fit you. If it is too wide, take in the side-seams, but *not* the centre-seam, as this would throw out the pleat. You can also make wider darts at the back and front until you have a snug fit round the waist and over the hips. Should it be too small, make the side-seams narrower and let out the darts.

To set in the pleat, fold inwards at each side back against the main body of the skirt. It should then be stitched across the top, and slip-stitched to the skirt with stitches that are not brought through to the right side of the material. When you have seamed all the main seams, stitched the darts, and pressed your work, turn the skirt right side out and, with tailor's chalk, draw two straight lines down the front of the skirt on either side of the centre-seam. Machine-stitch down these lines on the right side of the skirt, to give the centre-seam more strength.

The top of the pleat may be finished with a straight bar or with a silk arrow-head. To make a bar, satin-stitch[1] about an inch across the top of the pleat and at right angles to it, taking care to keep your stitches of an even length. This strengthens the top of pleat and will prevent it tearing if you should jump on a bus with too long a stride. A hand-stitched arrow-head[2] can be as useful, and though it takes longer to do is more decorative.

A FROCK TO SUIT ANY WOMAN

There is no doubt that blouses and skirts are the most economical way of dressing, as you can have so many changes for so small a cost. For instance, three skirts and half-a-dozen blouses, provided they are made up in colours and materials that can all be worn with each other, will give you eighteen different changes of costume. However, many women will not wear them because they say they are too fat, too thin, or stick out at the wrong places. So here's a pattern for a frock that will suit all types and sizes of figure. The V-neck, slightly gathered bodice, and full, but not too full skirt, will suit and flatter young and old. It can be made with long or short sleeves.

The measurements of the frock for the average figure are: 40 inches long, 34-inch bust, 28-inch waist, and a 38-inch hip. If you need a larger bust measurement, or a wider hip or waist measurement, the extra inches are given by making the pattern the required number of inches wider at the point where you need extra fullness. To make it smaller, take in a larger seam allowance and adjust to fit with darts.

The pattern is cut from a rectangle of paper according to the diagram given. Each little square on the diagram represents 1 inch. Mark the points on your piece of paper by measuring straight across it from the centre-front, then draw in the outlines of the pattern. Don't forget also to mark in any darts indicated. For a short-sleeved dress you will need $3\frac{1}{2}$ yards of 36-inch material, and 4 yards for long sleeves. Use tailor's chalk to mark in the outlines of the pattern, and compare your own pattern carefully with that given in the diagram to see that your curves are graduated correctly, and your straight lines drawn at the right angle.

For this frock, buy a material that will drape softly, as there are small pleats in the front of the bodice and darts at the sleeve tops, so you want a material that will fall gracefully and not be

[1] See p. 114.   [2] See p. 56.

too thick or too stiff to handle. Suggestions are fine woollen, artificial silk or rayon, marocain, cloque or wool jersey.

When you have made the pattern, take the material and fold it in half lengthwise (iron out the creases first, please), and place the pieces of the pattern on it according to the diagram. Keep them all as close together as possible so that there is no waste of material.

MAKING UP THE FROCK

To make up the frock, the blouse and skirt sections should be put together first. Start with the front bodice and front skirt. Lay the pieces out flat on a table, and pin the two sections together, the top of the skirt overlapping the bodice. Pin the bodice into even pleats on either side of the point of the skirt yoke to make it fit. Don't snip bits of the bodice side-seams away because you think the bodice is too big ; alter the width of the little pleats till the sides of the bodice fall exactly into line with the sides of the skirt. Then pin up the back sections in the same way, the top of the skirt turned under and laid over the bodice section. Tack all this up, then join the side-seams, leaving an opening on the left-hand side of the dress 8 inches long—2 inches above the waist-seam and 6 inches below it. This makes the placket.

The neck, sleeves and hem are bound with bias binding (or Prussian binding for the hem). One word of advice about binding. Never put a silk binding on to the hem of a wool skirt ; always use a cotton one. The reason for this is that the wool is heavier than the silk, and the silk binding with the extra weight on it will gradually split or rot long before the dress is anything like worn out. Put a cotton binding on in the first place so that you don't have to re-bind later.

A COATEE FOR SPRING AND AUTUMN

Have you ever considered wearing a coatee or jacket over your dress when the weather is mild, but not mild enough to go out without a coat ? You may not be able to afford an extra full-length, light-weight coat for spring and early autumn in war-time, but a coatee or jacket worn over your frock takes only $2\frac{1}{2}$ yards of 36-inch material and will give you the extra warmth you need.

This is the way to make a neat, collarless jacket. Use your basic bodice pattern.[1] Your original foundation pattern is 19 inches long, but you will need a depth of 26 inches for a jacket, and the width at the bottom of the centre-front should be 15 inches. When you are cutting the pattern for the jacket

[1]See p. 22.

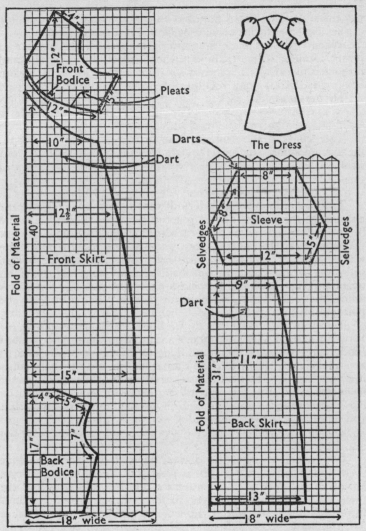

The Dress

9. PATTERN FOR AN ALL-PURPOSE DRESS.

at both back and front, draw a line slanting outwards from the 19-inch length at the waist-line to a length of 26 inches at the hip-line, and 15 inches across on both pieces.

You also need two pieces of facing for the front of the jacket. These go just inside the two front sections, neaten them, and give you a double thickness of material on which to make buttonholes.

To cut the facings, take your front bodice pattern, and measure in 5 inches from the point of the neck-line at the centre-front. Draw a straight line from top to bottom of the pattern through this point. This gives you the outline for your facing. It is, actually, an exact section of the front bodice pattern.

To make up the jacket, join the side-seams and shoulder-seams and adjust to fit you. The facing is put on right side to right side, seamed down from the curve of the neck-line along the two fronts of the bodice. The seam is then pressed open, the facing folded in, and the whole thing pressed flat on the wrong side.

PATCH POCKETS FOR YOUR JACKET

This jacket looks very well with patch pockets. To make the pattern for the pockets, cut a piece of paper 7½ inches wide and 8 inches deep (these measurements allow for turnings). When you have cut two pockets from your material, turn under the raw edges ¼ inch all round and tack. When you have tacked, press the turnings flat, as this will help you to avoid bulkiness when you are putting the pockets on to the jacket. Then tack them into position. They should be placed 3 inches up from the bottom of the jacket hem, and 2 inches along from the side-seams of the jacket.

It is a good idea to trace round the pockets with tailor's chalk before you tack them on. Then look at your chalk tracings and make quite sure that they are even on both sides, exactly the same distance from the hem, and exactly the same distance from the side-seams. If you have turned in more material on one pocket than on another, unpick the tackings and start again. It will drive your friends mad if you walk about with uneven pockets on your jacket, and give away the fact that you're a poor and impatient dressmaker.

When you have got the pockets accurately placed, machine them round on the right side as closely to the edge as you can. If you're not very good at accurate machine-stitching and the lines are wavy, you can cover these up by buying a length of braid and sewing it round the edge of the pockets by hand as a trimming.

A SWING JACKET FOR THE FULLER FIGURE

For those who are too short and plump, and too broad across the bust and hips for a fitted jacket, here is a pattern for a swing-back coatee which may be found more suitable to their figure requirements.

Use the front section of the bodice for the two front pieces, and making them 30 inches long (finger-tip length). Two godets have to be cut to insert down the centre-back of the coatee to give it a swing-back effect. Cut out a rectangle of paper 30 inches long and 9 inches wide. At the top of the rectangle mark in 2½ inches each side. Then from the bottom corner each side of the rectangle cut in a straight slanting line right up to the two points you have already marked 2½ inches in at the top. Cut two pieces of pattern like this in the material to be inserted in the centre-back.

When you come to cut out the back bodice for the coatee, you will find that the centre-back line is dead straight, and not cut on the slant like the edge of the godets. This line, therefore, must be slanted in the centre so that it fits perfectly on to the edge of the godet. To do this, when you come to cut the material, place the godet pattern beneath the pattern for the bodice back, and slant the centre line in accordance with the line of the godet. You will, at the same time, get the correct length for the back. If you are cutting out the back bodice on the fold of the material, cut down the centre fold and then slope the sides.

The godets are then joined together down each long side, and then the two sides left free are joined to each side of the centre-back. Join the side-seams and the shoulder-seams. The neck binding is carried right down the front of the coatee to the hem at both sides.

DO YOU LIKE BELL SLEEVES?

The basic sleeve pattern[1] which has already been given will fit this coatee, but you may prefer to have a loose bell-like finish at the wrist with the loose coatee. To get this, when you cut out the sleeve pattern, instead of cutting in towards the wrist so that the bottom of the sleeve measures 8 inches across, cut outwards from the elbow so that it measures 14 inches across at the bottom.

Press out the inside seams of this jacket as you go, and then take a little extra time and bind them at the edges with Prussian binding, so that not only do they not fray, but you can take the coat off without being self-conscious about it.

HINTS FOR THE DRESSMAKER

HERE are some professional tips to help you to give your own dressmaking a well-finished look.

Seams of all unlined coats and jackets should be bound with Prussian binding the same colour as the material. The binding is machined to the raw edge of the seam, turned under and slip-stitched to it.

[1] See p. 39.

Seams of frocks and of blouses in fine wool can be " pinked." This means cutting little triangles out of the seam at regular intervals to prevent it fraying, in the same way as you snip a triangle out of the end of a small girl's hair-ribbon to stop it fraying. If you have a pair of pinking shears (which cost about a guinea), you cut only along the seam edges before you open them to press them flat, and the shears, having serrated edges, do the work for you. Pinking shears save a great deal of time, but they are expensive, so if you are going to do a lot of sewing, and your neighbours are needlewomen too, consider getting a pair between you. It is unlikely you will all want to " pink " at the same time.

Seams on very fine materials such as silk, silk jersey, rayon, cloqué or marocain should always be overcast.

All seams, on all types of material, provided the seam allowance is wide enough, can be turned under and machine-stitched down to neaten them. Neatening of seams is a very important part of dressmaking, as it gives a good professional finish to have your seam edges made properly tidy.

TO PRESS PLEATS SUCCESSFULLY

When you are pressing pleats in a skirt or frock, put an odd piece of the fabric, or a thick piece of brown paper, beneath the pleat edge. This will prevent the edge from being pressed down too hard on to the main section of the garment and leaving a mark. Pleats should first be pressed very gently on the right side of the material over a dry cloth with a fairly damp one on top of it. In this way you won't get too much moisture through and mark the material. The pleats should then be pressed firmly over a damp cloth on the wrong side.

Use your sleeve-board not only for sleeves but also for pointed yokes, neck edges, tucks and gathers on a bodice. These little fiddling bits of pressing are more easily accomplished on a narrow board such as a sleeve board.

TO MATCH UP PATTERNED PIECES

If you are using checked or striped material, unless you have bought a special pattern to give the correct yardage, allow another half-a-yard extra on the usual yardage you buy. Material often has to be cut to waste on striped or check designs because the pattern must be adjusted so that stripes all run the same way and checks meet each other exactly, not a little above or below each other.

When cutting out striped material, place your bodice and skirt patterns so that the centre-fold comes exactly on the middle of a stripe or in the centre of a check. If you are putting in godets or a pointed yoke on to a bodice, lay the pieces of the pattern which have to be tacked up on the right side so that you get the design in alignment.

To do this, turn under the seam allowance on the largest main section and carefully pin over on to the smaller section so that stripe meets stripe, and check accurately overlies check. Pin down at inch intervals, putting in the pin at right angles to the way the stripe is running. Then slip-tack, still on the right side. Slip-tacking is done in the same way as slip-stitching, only taking much larger stitches. Working on the right side of the material, put your needle underneath the top piece and take a tiny stitch into the bottom piece, then slide the needle along half-an-inch or more and bring it through the top. The garment is then machined by turning on to the wrong side, and folding the top piece of material back flat so that you can get at the seam edges.

HOW TO TREAT VELVET

You may be ambitious enough to make a velvet frock or coatee. There are two things to remember here. The first is to lay all your pieces of pattern on the material so that they are running the same way, i.e. the way of the pile. If you are not sure which way the pile runs, hold the length of velvet vertically up to the light—now turn it upside down and hold it to the light again. Whichever way shows the surface to be *darker* is the way the pile runs. Bodice, skirt, sleeve pattern pieces *must* all lie in the same direction.

Secondly, the matter of pressing. Velvet, of course, cannot be pressed as other materials or you flatten the pile, and can never raise it again. The only way to press open seams is to stand your iron upright (using not too hot an iron) and draw the back of the seam gently, bit by bit, up and down the point of the iron. Try to get a couple of people to help you with the long seams, so that they can hold the seam out taut while you run the point of the iron along it on the wrong side of the material. Another thing to remember is that velvet creases and marks very easily, and therefore needs delicate handling when you are making it up. It is a good plan to make yourself a couple of little velvet finger-stalls from odd snippings of the material, so that when it has to be handled firmly for drawing the seams over the iron, your fingers do not leave marks on it.

If the velvet becomes crushed in the making, put a wet cloth over a very hot iron, and bring the iron down within half-an-inch of the creased part. The steam will raise the creased or crushed pile. Be very careful to avoid getting any drops of water on the material itself.

TO KEEP YOUR WORK LOOKING FRESH

Finally, when you are dressmaking don't stuff your work into your work-box or basket with socks to be mended and collars that need turning. Keep it in an old dress-box. Those nice flat boxes that come home from the cleaners are admirable for this. The pieces of the garment can then be laid flat in it and all kept together. If there is any tissue paper in the box, so much the better. Fold it over these to prevent it creasing. For a garment to look creased and shabby before you have worn it even once is really most discouraging.

When you've got the shoulder-seams machined, the skirt seamed to the bodice, and your garment only awaits the finishing-off at neck, wrists and hem, it should be hung up on a coat-hanger, and covered with a dust-proof cover.

If you are working on a light material in some delicate pastel shade, always work with a piece of clean white sheeting, or an old face-towel on the table or on your lap. Even the cleanest of us get dust on our clothes. Take great care to keep your sewing spotlessly clean and uncreased, then, when it is finished, you will have the satisfaction of hearing one of your friends say, " Goodness me, I'd never have believed hands had touched it."

TRICKS FOR SMARTNESS

THERE are many tricks of the trade in dressmaking which, far from being intricate to learn, are very simple short-cuts to that neat professional finish which always looks as though it has taken hours of skilled workmanship.

The first and most important trick is to keep your iron hot from the moment you start cutting out, and use it to press every seam as you go along. The material should be ironed flat before you start cutting it, as the fold ridges and creases in it all lessen your chance of getting a completely accurate fit to a garment.

HEMS THE EXPERT USES

Clumsy hems are often the bane of the amateur dressmaker. These can be avoided in various ways. If you are turning up the hem of a skirt, unless you are working on thin silk or chiffon, always use Prussian binding. This is a flat binding like tape, and should be machine-stitched to the raw edge of the skirt on the right side. Then when the hem is turned up it is easy to slip-stitch along the binding. This avoids the double fold of material at the top of the hem, which looks so bulky and betrays the amateur.

When you're dealing with a circular skirt, machine on the Prussian binding and leave the skirt to hang overnight to give it a chance to sag. Turn up the hem with the skirt lying flat on a table. See that seam meets seam. Where there is too much fullness pin in little darts on the wrong side of the material at right angles to the hem. The final hemming should be done with very loose stitches, otherwise it will pucker and make a ridge on the right side.

When you're tacking long seams try to work at a deal table so that you can pin your work to the edge of the table, and you'll then find if you hold the material stretched out towards you you'll get along much quicker.

A TRICK TO AVOID THE WAVY HEM

Wavy hems on silk or any thin materials are another betrayal of the amateur. These can be avoided by an easy little trick which looks like a bias binding finish, but is easier and quicker to do. Turn the material up about half-an-inch on the right side, and seam it along close to the edge with small running-stitches. Then turn the raw edge of the garment over and under on to the wrong side and hem it down, taking care to place your stitches through the little seam but not all the way through on to the right side of the material.

TACKING TO SAVE TIME AND TROUBLE

Never, never pull tacking threads out of a garment by their full length. Snip them at intervals and then draw them out gently, otherwise you may pull the garment out of shape. The edges of garments cut on the cross, and all edges of fine fabrics, should be tacked to thin paper as soon as they are cut out. This will prevent stretching and pulling out of shape. If it seems a nuisance, remember it is a professional trick, and saves endless trouble later.

When pressing out seams on very thick materials soap the edges. The hot iron will melt the soap and stick the seam down flat. This is an especially good tip for the seams of skirts made from heavy tweed.

TO MAKE A SKIRT HANG WELL

Skirts, and especially flared skirts, are often difficult to make hang correctly. The usual fault lies at the waist-line, and not in the cut of the skirt itself. A too loose waist-line will cause the skirt either to drop at the sides or flare out into fullness at the knees.

When you try the skirt on, be sure the waist fits snugly. The wider the bottom of the skirt, the deeper should be the width of petersham you sew into the waist. Two or three inches is the correct width for a medium or narrow skirt, but a really wide, flared skirt should have a waist-band four or five inches deep. If you are sure the waist is well fitting and the skirt still drops, lift it up at the front waist-line an inch or so higher than at the back. Do this on a flat surface. If it drops at the back, the trouble can be remedied by placing darts about 4 inches deep at each side of the back. One dart each side should be enough.

DIFFICULTIES IN MAKING DARTS

Darts are another snare for the beginner. A professional always tacks her darts into place before they are sewn. She also works down towards the point of the dart, tapering it off gradually, and keeping the last four or five stitches parallel to the edge of the dart. This ensures that it is flat on the right side. Darts should always be cut open down the centre, once they are in the right position and seamed, and then pressed out flat.

TO ACHIEVE A SMART SHOULDER-LINE

A badly-fitting shoulder-line on an otherwise well-made garment will ruin it. As the shoulder-lines of individuals vary so much, it is worth knowing how to get a correct and smart look to your shoulders.

People with wide shoulders should place the top of their paper pattern about an inch-and-a-half away from the centre fold to lengthen the line. The neck can be made to fit by taking small tucks or darts in the pattern.

Narrow or sloping shoulders can be fitted and built up by taking in rather more seam at the top of the arm-hole, and then padding with horsehair pads, which can be bought for a few pence at any draper's, and which are specially made for this purpose. Most shoulder-lines, except in very thin materials, look better if they are padded. The pad is tacked in between the shoulder and arm-hole seams, and then stitched in finally when the arm-hole fullness has been adjusted.

TAILORING TRICKS WORTH KNOWING

ALL these are tricks known to every dressmaker, and should be in constant use by the home dressmaker when she is making frocks or lingerie. Tailoring, however, and tailored finishes are usually more intricate but are worth learning because, even if you fight shy of making yourself a coat or a suit, you should know how to re-line an old coat or jacket, how to finish a placket neatly, and how to make bound buttonholes. You will save yourself delay as well as expense if you can do these jobs yourself.

HOW TO COPY A COAT LINING

Coat linings are not difficult. Cut your new one from the pattern of the old one. You'll need about 5 yards of 36-inch wide material, or $2\frac{1}{2}$ yards for a half-lining. First join the side-seams, then laying the coat flat on a table tack the lining into it, seam to seam. Remember two things. Make a soft, unpressed pleat right down the centre-back, and two small pleats of the same type below each shoulder in front. These pleats prevent the lining from dragging, and should be about $1\frac{1}{2}$ inches wide. Never attach your lining to the hem of a coat. Turn it up neatly and allow it to hang loose.

If you are lining a previously unlined garment, make a pattern from the coat from paper. You'll need three pieces, one for the back, and one for each of the side fronts, in addition to the sleeve pieces, if the sleeves are also to be lined. Pin your paper on to the coat, which should be laid out flat, then cut round it about an inch beyond the coat seams. A lining should be larger than the coat, as you have to allow for easing and turnings. The important thing is not to forget the unpressed pleats.

A NEAT AND HARD-WEARING PLACKET

Plackets are a tailoring job. Having left an opening of about 8 inches deep on the left-hand side of your garment, be very careful not to handle it more than is necessary, as plackets have a habit of stretching and, if this occurs, will later bulge on the figure. If the material you are working on is closely woven, use it to bind the placket. If it is a loosely-woven material which frays easily, you would do better to use a piece of dark sateen.

For the front side of the placket, cut on the cross a strip $\frac{3}{4}$ inch wide, and the length of your placket, plus $\frac{1}{2}$-inch turnings at top and bottom. Tack it, wrong side out, to the raw edge of the right side of the material. Machine it on, turn it over, and catch it down to the body of the garment, on the wrong side, with neat slip-stitches.

The back of the placket is the piece that goes underneath. Cut out across the side-seam turning about an inch below the bottom of the placket hole. Then cut out on the straight a piece of material about 2 inches wide and 1 inch longer than your placket opening. Stitch it to the raw edge of the skirt, leaving the extra inch loose at the bottom of the placket hole. Now fold under and sew exactly as for the front placket edge. Lay the skirt flat with the placket edges together, front overlapping back, pin, turn inside out and sew down the loose bottom edge of the back. It can be strengthened with a thin bar of close oversewing. You will now find that your placket overlaps neatly and fits without bulging.

On very thin materials a simpler kind of placket is sometimes used. To make this, cut out a 2-inch wide strip of material, long enough to go all round the placket hole, allowing for turnings at the top and easing in at the bottom. Pin it, right side to right side, to the edges of the placket hole. At the bottom it must be eased in by making tiny pleats, to be pressed flat on the wrong side. Machine-stitch the strip on, then turn it inside and slip-stitch, as for an ordinary placket.

When it comes to sewing on the press-studs, put them on the back placket first, then mark their heads with a piece of chalk. Press them down on to the front placket and they'll leave little white marks which will show exactly where the corresponding studs should be placed.

TO BIND BUTTONHOLES EXPERTLY

When you are making bound buttonholes, decide on the right length for them before cutting the material. They should be about $\frac{1}{4}$ inch wider than the diameter of the button. Mark the position of them with tailor's chalk or a tacking thread.

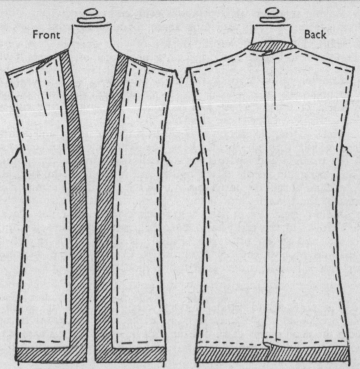

Front   Back

10. *To prevent it dragging, a coat lining should be cut larger than the garment for which it is required. The extra fullness is formed into loose pleats, one on each shoulder and one in the centre of the back.*

A tacking thread is safer, as you then mark the wrong side of the material at the same time.

Cut a piece of binding material on the cross 2 inches wide and the length of the buttonhole, plus an inch at each end, i.e. 3 inches across by 2 inches deep. Put this right side down on the right side of the material, and tack into position so that the centre of the binding falls exactly on to the tacking thread already marked. Stitch firmly by hand or machine all the way round the tacking thread and about ¼ inch away from it. Then cut a clean line right through the binding and the material along the length of your tacking thread. At the end of the line snip across diagonally to the stitching on either side, and pull the binding through the opening on to the wrong side of your material. It should then be turned under and hemmed flat all round the buttonhole. The extra material is dealt with by making small inverted pleats at each end on the wrong side. Press the buttonholes and tack them together till your work is finished, to prevent them stretching.

THE ARROW-HEADED PLEAT

Another tailoring trick which is often used as a trimming is to make silk arrow-heads to strengthen and decorate pleats in frocks or skirts. These can be made in a contrasting silk if you wish them to be more than usually decorative.

Mark a triangle in chalk at the top of the pleat, and bring your needle through the back of the bottom left-hand corner of the triangle and up to take a small stitch in the top point. Then bring the needle down again and insert it in the bottom right-hand corner of the triangle, take a large stitch through the back of the triangle, and bring your needle out up through the left-hand corner. From there you stitch into the top point again, then down to the right-hand corner, across into the left-hand corner, and so on until the triangle is filled. This makes a neat and professional-looking finish to any tailored pleat, and prevents it from tearing. It will also hide a tear in a pleat.

THE SECRETS OF HANDLING FUR

The cutting and repair of fur is really a job for the expert, but occasionally you may wish to make a fur collar at home from the good pieces of an old fur coat or stole. In this case it is not worth the expense of having it done by a furrier, and with a little care you can do it successfully yourself.

The chief thing is to be careful not to cut the hairs of the fur, and to place and piece the fur so that all the hairs are running the same way. Never use scissors. Always cut with a razor-blade or sharp knife, through the pelt from the back.

Stretch the skin, fur side downwards, on to a pastry board, and tack the edges down with light tacks. Place your collar pattern on the pelt and mark in the outlines with chalk. Then cut round the chalk marks with firm, short slashes, cutting only about an inch at a time, and being very watchful to cut only the pelt and to avoid cutting or tearing the hairs.

To piece the collar together, put the fur sides facing each other and join up at the back with small, firm overcasting stitches through the pelt only. To avoid catching the hairs up when you are sewing, put a thin piece of cardboard between the two fur sides and work closely over the top of it.

The outside edges of the collar are finished off with tape or Prussian binding. This is laid along the edge of the skin on the fur side, firmly oversewn with small stitches, and then turned over and caught up lightly into the pelt at the back.

ACCESSORIES COSTING NEXT-TO-NOTHING

HOWEVER much, or however little money a woman may spend on clothes, she will attain quiet distinction and individuality in her dressing only if she pays attention to detail. You should choose shoes, gloves, bags and buttonholes not only to complete the picture, but so that with these and other accessories you can still look smart when you're wearing a garment you've had for years.

Keep yourself well dressed by buying or making clothes of good material and classical cut, and dressing them up with ingeniously-chosen accessories that will give them an air of distinction and put them in the front line of fashion at little cost of money or coupons.

TO SAVE MONEY ON ACCESSORIES

There should be basic accessories in your dressing-table drawers, just as there are basic garments in your wardrobe. Try and keep a good pair of gloves, purse and shoes all matching that will go with most of your clothes, and for these pay as much as you can afford. What you pay for these things is entirely a personal matter, but one set of good, well-made accessories will give you a better-dressed air than several cheap sets.

For instance, suppose you choose nut-brown as the basic colour of your winter wardrobe, and decide to have a green frock for the spring, and for summer, prints of green, brown, butterscotch and maize yellow. You may foolishly buy for yourself a bright-red handbag, and a brown one and a green one for your winter and spring outfits, paying as little for them as possible. When summer comes round you're confronted with a problem, but the green bag looks cool, though shabby. So you get a biscuit-coloured or white one for the summer.

By now you've spent enough on bags to have provided yourself at first with one good hogskin one, which would have been much more clever. For this will wear, you can sponge it over lightly with soap-suds and very little warm water, and polish it up with white shoe-cream. You can have gloves to match it, which you can wash at home on your hands. When summer comes this glove and purse set will still look what it is— elegant and good. Similarly, if you're wearing navy in winter, get a good navy leather handbag and gloves that will still look right with the dusty pink linen dress you're going to make for warmer weather.

A good rule is to buy accessories that *match each other* and that pick up the predominant colour in your wardrobe. Then you'll never look " all bits and pieces." And what is more, you won't waste money.

TOUCHES TO EXPRESS YOUR PERSONALITY

If you're a person who loves colour, gaiety and individuality, you may be thinking this all sounds very dull—hardy, perennial clothes and good plain accessories, preferably in a dark colour. But accessories don't mean just gloves, bags and shoes, they mean belts, buttonholes, scarves, bracelets, collar and cuff sets— all the small decorative details that make one outfit different from another, one woman smart and another woman dowdy, and it is in the choice and the making of these that you stamp your own personality on your clothes.

A POCHETTE TO MATCH YOUR DRESS TRIMMINGS

Make a pochette in felt to match your dress trimmings, or in a piece of the material left over from your frock. You need only $\frac{3}{8}$ of a yard ($13\frac{1}{2}$ inches) of 36-inch material. You will also need $\frac{3}{8}$ of a yard of buckram. It costs about 1/9 a yard. From these you can make a pochette 12 inches wide and 9 inches deep, large enough to carry make-up, keys, hankie, and the couple of bills or letters that always seem to be in every woman's handbag.

Cut your buckram into a rectangle 27 inches long by 12 inches wide. Then lay it on a flat surface over your length of material, which should be cut 28 inches long by 10 inches wide. The extra inch of material is used for $\frac{1}{2}$-inch turnings all round. Turn the material in and tack it evenly all round the edges of the buckram, as close in as you can. Be careful to keep it well and evenly stretched across the buckram, and don't let the tacking stitches come through again on to the material. Still keeping the whole thing laid out flat, cut a lining from $\frac{3}{8}$ of a yard of dark sateen or from any odd dark pieces you may have in your piece-bag.

The lining should be turned under all round and hemmed, pressed on the wrong side, laid over the buckram and over the tacked edges of the material, and lightly pinned into place. Join it carefully to the edges of the material that are overlapping the buckram, to cover the tacks, and stitch with invisible slip-stitches.

Now fold the whole thing into three equal parts, each 9 inches deep. The first two sections make the bag, the top one is the overlap. The sides are joined on the outside with close, tight, small oversewing stitches in the same coloured thread as the material, so that they do not show. Sew on a couple of press-studs just inside the two top corners of the overlap. Mark the points of these with chalk and press down on to the body of the bag, so that you have the exact position on which to sew the other halves of the studs.

FRILLS AND JABOTS FOR DAINTINESS

Collar and cuff sets are easy to make at home, so are jabots, and these are the things that give daintiness to the most simple frock. Try making a toby frill of stiff black tulle sewn double, for the neck of a black dress. Bind it with white or pale-pink satin baby ribbon at the outside edges, and make 7-inch deep gauntlets to match, for the wrists of your dress. For a toby frill you require $\frac{3}{4}$ yard of tulle. Double it lengthwise and cut it in a semi-circle 7 inches deep and the width of the neck-line of your frock. The inside edges of the frill should be bound together with black ribbon, or a wide black silk shoe lace. The outside edges are cut open, and both edges bound with the pastel ribbon. Make the gauntlets in the same way, using $\frac{2}{3}$ yard of tulle.

A pleated jabot that will look as though it came direct from Paris can be made from a quarter of a yard of white piqué, white muslin or fine cambric.

Turn under the edges of your material all round, sew a fine hem, and lay the material lengthwise on a flat surface. Then make a gauge for your pleats from a post card. Mark an inch measure on your post-card, and fold the pleats into the right width by means of this marker. The first pleat should be folded away from you, the next towards you. Continue down the whole strip of the material, pinning each pleat as you go with pins inserted to lie at right angles to the pleat. When the whole thing is pinned, tack the pleats down with diagonal tacks. Diagonal tacks are made by putting your needle into the top pleat (the one farthest away from you) on the right of the pleat, and tacking down towards the left of the pleat. The next stitch is made directly under it, and so on, and you push the jabot up and away from you as you proceed.

The pleats are sewn down by hand from behind, taking care not to bring your needle through on to the right side as you join them to each other. To make the collar for the jabot, cut two half-circles of the same material. These are sewn under the jabot at the front two edges. The back edges are finished off as though for the front of a collar, and lie flat down the back. It is quite a good idea to fasten the collar at the back with a small press-stud, then you need not attach any of it to the dress, but simply put it round your neck and clip it together at the back. The jabot is allowed to hang loose down the front of the dress.

TASSELS TO TRIM YOUR SHOULDER-LINE

Have you any left-over pieces of brightly-coloured wool? If so, turn them into tassels, and sew them along the shoulder-lines of your dress to make military-looking epaulettes.

To make tassels, cut a piece of cardboard the depth you want the tassel to be, and wind the wool round and round it about fifteen times. Then knot the strands together at the top, and cut the ends open at the bottom. Take a piece of firm silk of the same colour (or a colour that contrasts well) and wind this several times round the tassel just below the knotted threads at the top to make the head of the tassel. Sew the tassels along the shoulder-line of your dress at regular intervals. About five tassels on each shoulder are enough.

HOME-MADE SCARVES ARE INEXPENSIVE

Scarves can be made from ¼ yard of 36-inch wide material, and fringed at the ends in the same way as for ribbon fringes. Or for a winter scarf in fine wool make little tassels to go on the end. For these tassels the wool should be wound round the cardboard gauge only about half-a-dozen times, as you don't want them to be too thick. It is much less expensive to buy a length of plain or check wool, flowered or plain silk, than to buy scarves ready-made, and if you make fringed or tasselled ends to them they won't look home-made.

GLOVES THAT HAVE THAT EXPENSIVE LOOK

You can make your own gloves from felt. Cut a pattern from a pair of old ones, and join the fingers and thumbs together with stab-stitch[1] on the right side. Choose cream-coloured felt and stitch them in nut-brown, and you'll have a pair of gloves that look really expensive. The gussets between the fingers should be put in between the two sides of the gloves before the sides are joined, and these are seamed in by fine oversewing, still on the right side.

BOWS FOR BELT AND SLEEVES

Another use for odd pieces of ribbon is to make them into bows. These can be sewn in couples, one above the other, on the edge of a short sleeve or at the front of a belt. To make ribbon bows, fold each end over into the required length and sew flat. Trim the ends. The middle of the bow is then finished

[1] See p. 115.

by taking a few running-stitches down the centre of it to draw it up, and folding over it another piece of ribbon with a small pleat down the centre. Hem down neatly at the back.

All these are the kinds of things that need very little trouble, cost next-to-nothing, but will give an air of distinction and an expensive look to quite ordinary clothes.

ACCESSORIES FROM YOUR PIECE-BAG

NEVER throw away any odd pieces of material, as some kind of decorative or useful purpose can always be found for them. A well-ordered piece-bag will save you many odd pence from time to time, and will do much to relieve the monotony of a rationed wardrobe.

It is better to store pieces in a large square cardboard hat-box than in a bag. If you put odd pieces of material, lengths of ribbon, buttons and buckles into a large bag they will get crumpled and " mussed," the buckles are likely to tear delicate fabrics, the buttons drop to the bottom of the bag and get lost, and the bits of material become really dishearteningly crumpled. So find a large box, and get your bits and pieces into order.

Fine materials of delicate weave like chiffon, silk, satin, suzette, and muslin should always be rolled together, and tied round with a piece of cotton. Heavier fabrics are best folded as flat as possible and laid at the bottom of the box on top of each other. Lengths of ribbon should also be rolled, and fastened with a couple of stitches so that they don't come undone. Don't put pins into them for these will tear the other fabrics you are storing.

It is worth while stringing buttons together on a length of double thread. This will keep them all together, and it takes up less room than putting them into little boxes. Buckles should also be strung together and wrapped in an odd piece of material so that the spikes of them do not tear delicate fabrics. When you are throwing garments away always cut off the buttons and any fastenings such as press studs, hooks and eyes, and slide fasteners. If you are storing odd pieces of lamé or brocade, or any tinsel threaded fabric, wrap them in a piece of black or dark-blue tissue paper to prevent them tarnishing.

A RIBBON COLLAR FROM ODDMENTS

If you have odd lengths of ribbons that are not long enough to make rosettes, or not all of the same colour or width, here is something you can do with them to make an original and delightful trimming for the neck of a dark dress. Cut the ribbon into four to five-inch lengths, and sew them on to a piece of

ordinary tape at three-inch intervals so that they hang down.
Then tack the tape just inside the neck-line of your frock. The
ribbon will hang over the neck-line like a collar, and the more
different colours you have, the prettier it will be. The ribbons
should be either all the same width all round, or of two or three
widths arranged alternately.

USE YOUR INITIALS AS A TRIMMING

An odd piece of felt, highly-coloured woollen material, or
stiff bright taffeta can be used to cut your initials from. Whip
the edges unless you are using felt, mount the initials on a piece
of canvas, or petersham for stiffening, and pin them just below
the left-hand shoulder of your dress, on your coat lapel, your
bag, or even on the side of your hat.

A PLEATED BOW GIVES A SMART FINISH

A wide width of ribbon, a piece of taffeta or any fairly stiff
material can be used up to make a pleated bow for the front of a
frock. Pleat carefully, and stitch the pleats down at the back as
you go along. Then twist a piece of cotton round the centre of
the pleated length so that it makes a fan-shape each end by
drawing the pleats tightly together in the middle. Cover this
centre piece with a tiny end of ribbon or velvet, and pin on to
the front of your dress just under the chin.

ODDS AND ENDS FOR BELTS, POSIES AND COLLARS

Have you any braid left over from curtains ? The white or
cream braid with tasselled ends will make lovely belts for a dark
frock. Fasten a buckle on to one end, and put the braid round
your waist so that the tassels hang down. From furnishing chintz
left-overs you can make posies by cutting round the shape of
the flowers and mounting them on canvas. They also look
well appliqued on to a piece of dark material and used to make
a collar and cuff set.

Don't despise pieces of lingerie silk for collars and cuffs.
If you haven't enough to cut a whole collar or enough depth to
make cuffs, cut the odd pieces of material into narrow strips on
the cross, whip the edges and use them for frilling sewn inside
the neck of your frock, and just inside the wrists. Pale pink
chiffon gathered on to the neck and wrist-lines of a black dress
gives a most attractive effect.

Larger pieces of material can be made up into scarves,
shoulder-capes (cut a semi-circle for a cape and bind the edges),
sleeveless fronts to wear beneath a jacket instead of a blouse,
turbans and posies. And any piece of material, however small,
will some day come in useful to mend a tear or put on a patch.

MAKE MORE OF OLD CLOTHES

MOST of us at one time or another have been faced with the position of having a wardrobe of perfectly good clothes, and yet having "nothing to wear." We're tired of one garment, the elbows are wearing thin on another, and our favourite-coloured frock now has an old-fashioned neck-line.

Now that clothing is rationed, however, this sort of situation must never occur. You simply must take the trouble to "vet" your clothes regularly. Go over them weekly, mend, clean and alter. Keep everything spruce and up-to-date and you'll never get tired of your clothes.

TO SMARTEN FRAYED WRISTS

You may have a good suit or frock that is frayed at the wrists. In the case of a suit the frayed edge will be on a fold. Cut it open right round the wrist, and cut away the frayed part, keeping the amount you cut off even all round. Then turn the edges in towards each other, the lower edge slightly beneath the top one, and slip-stitch together. Press over a damp cloth. Where you have to deal with a frayed wrist on a single thickness of material, cut off the frayed part and bind it with $\frac{1}{2}$-inch wide ribbon velvet to match the frock, or with wide braid in a dark colour.

INVISIBLE MENDING FOR A THREE-CORNERED SNAG

If you have been unlucky enough to catch your clothes on a sharp edge which has made a three-cornered tear, it can be mended almost invisibly by fish-bone stitch. Draw a thread from the selvedge of the garment, or from one of the seams where it will not show, and use this to mend the tear. Hold the edges of the material together on the wrong side of the garment, and put the needle in a little less than a quarter-of-an-inch from the edge. Pass it along under the cut and bring it up through the opposite edge at a slant and again at the same distance from the edge as before. Put the needle in again a little way from where it first went in and bring it across the underneath of the tear diagonally downwards, over the thread, and up through the opposite side, and so on. Hold the edges of the tear as tautly as you can between the left thumb and forefinger while you are mending it. Finish off with one or two small back-stitches at the end. Press the mend on the wrong side with a damp cloth and you will find it is scarcely noticeable.

PATCHES THAT WILL NEVER BE NOTICED

Sometimes a dress will go under the arms, tear at the placket-hole or rub very thin at the elbows, and you may be afraid to patch it in case it shows. If you patch with the same material, sew the patch with a thread drawn from the selvedge of the garment, and press it carefully afterwards, it should be unnoticed by any one except you. This type of patch should always be put *on the right side of the garment* so that there is no ridge to give it away.

Put the garment on a flat surface, right side out, and cut the patch much bigger than the hole it is to cover. Carefully match any design there may be, and if it is a plain material turn your patch about over the hole till the threads of the patch are running the way of the weave of the main garment. Turn under the patch edgings about half-an-inch all round and tack over the hole, then, holding the patch towards you, sew round the edges of patch and garment with neat small slip-stitches, using a thread drawn from the garment. Turn the whole thing over on to the wrong side and cut the turnings down to a quarter-of-an-inch, then overcast them to prevent them fraying. Press on the wrong side, taking special care to press with the point of the iron the stitches made on the right side, to flatten them.

TO PATCH WHERE SEAMS CROSS

If you have to patch a garment in a difficult place where seams cross, such as the underarms, it is a saving of time and patience to unpick the seams before you apply the patch. Cut the patch large enough to cover well beyond the hole or tear and the surrounding thin parts. Tack it firmly to the garment, and then cut it round to the shape of the hole or tear you are patching. Then cut away as much of the under, worn part as possible, so that when you re-seam the garment together you do not have three thicknesses of material in the cross-seams. Of course, if the hole or patch extends to both sides of the seam, you will have to make two separate patches.

TO STOP SHOULDER-STRAPS FROM STRAYING

Dress protectors should be washed each week and sewn back into place when they are quite dry. At the same time sew a little piece of tape into the shoulders of your dresses to catch up your shoulder-straps and prevent them slipping. The tape is sewn down each end near the neck, then fastened with press-studs at the shoulder end. This not only prevents the misery of groping in public for straying shoulder-straps, but will also prevent them breaking by being caught up over your arm when you bend down. Slip under the tape when you dress.

TO PREVENT OR CURE A BAGGY SKIRT

Skirts which bulge at the back are something we all know and deplore. This bulging can be prevented to a considerable extent by sewing a panel of artificial taffeta into the back of the skirt from the waist-band to three-quarters of the way down. The taffeta costs about 2/6 a yard and you need only half-a-yard. Sew it straight across, hemming it into the side-seams of the skirt. This will take the pull of your weight when you sit down.

If the skirt is already baggy, you can either shrink it at the back or lift the waist-line. To shrink it, turn the skirt inside out and pull it over a skirt board. Then take a piece of really wet muslin or cotton (without dressing in it), place it over the " seated " patch and press hard with a hot iron. If the bulge is too bad to respond to this shrinking, undo the waist-band at the back and lift the material up from $1\frac{1}{2}$ to 2 inches at the centre-back and cut it away. Then reset into the waist-band.

TO DARN A HOLE WHERE IT SHOWS

Burns or mothholes in the front of a skirt or bodice look neater if they are mended with invisible darning instead of with a patch. The two principal things needed for invisible darning are a good light and plenty of patience. The darning is done with the threads of the fabric itself, and these can usually be drawn from the hem of the skirt, any piece of inner facing or, if they are wide enough, from the seams. If you are working on a closely-woven fabric, choose a fine needle so that your darn is as near as possible in texture to the original weave. A thick or loosely-woven fabric should be darned with a thick needle. If you do it carefully no one but yourself will know it has been darned.

A FASHIONABLE TREATMENT FOR WORN ELBOWS

If elbows have worn thin on a dress, darn them on the wrong side of the garment with a thread drawn from one of the seams. Start the darn a good half-inch away from the thin patch to take the strain of the elbow pull and help it to lie flatter over the elbow itself.

If the elbows of a jacket have become worn, they can be covered by a triangle of suède or leather in a matching or contrasting colour. Many very expensive tweed or check suits have the elbows covered by these suède " patches." Odd bits of leather may be bought for a few pence from a leather merchant, or in many cases from your local Arts and Crafts shop. If you cannot get hold of any pieces, see if you have any old gloves and cut the wrist open flat. The patches are put on the right side of the garment with stab-stitch, done in a firm thread. Get a narrow strip of suède to sew round the back of the collar of your jacket so that it forms a trimming to match up to the elbow triangles.

A DARN THAT LOOKS LIKE KNITTING

It may be that your most attractive jumper has got a moth-hole in it where it shows most. In this case you will have to mend it by grafting so that it won't show. Thread a needle with a length of matching wool and run it along the garment just before the place where the stitches have gone. Put it through two stitches at the lower part of the hole, draw it through, and pick up another two stitches at the top of the hole, then down again into the lower stitches. Draw up tightly enough to fill the gap, but not so tightly as to put any strain on the main section of the garment. Grafting forms a line of imitation knitting that is non-detectable.

As long as a garment is not too far gone, neat efficient mending will give it a new lease of life. Repair where you can, and renovate where you can't.

TO TRANSFORM OLD CLOTHES

IF THE collar of your dress is worn and greasy, the underarms fluffy and split, the wrists frayed, and yet the skirt is still good, put a new yoke on that dress. Cut the top off just below the underarm, and then cut out a new yoke patterned on the one you have just cut off. You'll need about a yard-and-a-half of material. Buy a tartan or a dog's-tooth check or plaid for a plain dress. Try and get a fabric about the same weight as your dress—a silk top on heavy wool is obviously useless, as the skirt will drag the bodice out of shape. A material of similar weight and texture is easier to handle.

When you have put in the sleeves and joined the small side-seams, put the yoke on to the frock by tacking it straight across the back and front of the dress, keeping it absolutely flat and in a dead-straight line. Then machine-stitch it down about one-sixth of an inch from the edge. Make three or four close lines of machine-stitching each above the other to strengthen the hold of the yoke, and to give it a professional-looking finish.

WAISTCOATS GIVE NEW LIFE TO A FROCK

Another way of cheering up a good dress that you may be tired of is to make a couple of waistcoats for it. It takes only a yard of 36-inch material to make a sleeveless waistcoat. Cut it from your basic bodice pattern,[1] making it 22 inches deep at

[1] See p. 22.

the back and 26 inches deep at the front from top shoulder-line to hem. When you have cut it out, join up the shoulders and the side-seams, and bind the arm-holes, the front, neck-line and hem with braid or with coloured tape. You'll need about 3½ yards of this.

Round the corners of the bottom of the bodice pattern at the front before you turn up the hem. A velvet waistcoat looks charming with a plain woollen frock, and will dress it up for special occasions. For morning wear, waistcoats in checks or in a good bold colour look very cheerful and fresh.

NEW HALF-SLEEVES FOR A PLAIN DRESS

If you have a plain, one-coloured, long-sleeved dress that has become badly worn at wrists and elbows, but is still good at the underarms and neck, find a remnant of pretty, patterned silk, and make yourself new half-sleeves for it. The old sleeves should be cut off just above the elbow, and the new sleeves cut wide at the wrist. Cut the new sleeves from the pattern of the old ones, but widen them either side at the wrist-line. This fullness is gathered into a wrist-band, so that you have a full graceful sleeve. To make a tight sleeve for this purpose in contrasting material is apt to look like a renovation, but a full one, which utterly alters the style of the garment, will make your frock look like an entirely new model.

To make the little band into which you will gather the fullness of the material, cut a piece of the material 8 inches long and 4 inches wide. Then the sleeve wrist edges should be gathered to fit into the 8-inch band. Two rows of gathers are necessary to give the required fullness and make the set of the wrist more even. The rows should be made about a quarter-of-an-inch apart from each other, and then " stroked." To stroke the gathers, draw up the two threads as closely as possible, put a pin at the end of the gathering lines, and wind the loose threads round it. Then, using the eye of your needle, lift up each gather separately and push it towards your left thumb, pressing it firmly as you go. This takes time, but is worth it for the lovely, even, precise look of the gathers when it is done.

Loosen the two threads, and arrange the gathers evenly to fit the length of the wrist-band. Turn under the raw edge of the band, tack it down, and place it over the gathers on the right side of the sleeve. Then hem it on to the sleeve with tiny stitches, picking up a gather for each stitch as far as possible. Turn under the band on to the wrong side of the sleeve and, again turning under the raw edges, slip-stitch it down at the back, and press. The ends of the bands are finished off by turning them under, the under-side a little farther in than the top one, and slip-stitching together. Press, and sew on two small press-studs.

A SMART SKIRT FROM AN OLD COAT

You need a new skirt perhaps. And the coat you have had for three or four spring seasons really won't go on any longer. Make yourself a skirt from it. The parts you'll want to use for the skirt will be the parts that are least worn. If it is faded, turn the material inside out.

Cut your coat up close to the seams, and brush, clean and press the pieces of material before you cut them out. Cut the skirt from your basic pattern,[1] placing the pieces so that the hem of the skirt comes a little above where the hem of the coat had been. Hems are apt to fray, and the turn-up of the coat hem may have become worn. So it is wise not to have the hem of your new skirt in exactly the same place.

If your coat had a " flared " line, you will of course find it easier to make a flared or gored skirt. If it was a perfectly straight coat, make a straight skirt with an inverted pleat in front.

YOUR COAT MAY MAKE A BOLERO, TOO

After you have made your skirt, there is still enough of the coat left at the top for a sleeveless bolero. Take out the sleeves and remove any fur or trimming there may have been at the neck-line. Then cut straight across the back, and in a rounded curve where the two fronts meet, turn under and hem. You now have a skirt and a bolero from that old spring coat. Was it lined ? If it was, take the lining, wash it, and cut up a piece of it to line the back of your skirt half-way down. This is done by sewing a straight piece of material across the back of the skirt to the seam edges either side. It will take the pull when you sit down and prevent the skirt " sitting out."

Look in your wardrobe again. Have you a summer frock that is worn at the top ? Cut up the skirt of this and make yourself a short-sleeved blouse from it, to wear with the skirt and under the bolero. From two garments which you had considered more or less defunct you now have a completely new outfit for the early summer days.

TROUSERS MAKE A USEFUL SKIRT

Men's suitings make lovely skirts for women, as the weave of the cloth is so strong, and the materials used for men's suits are often so much smarter than women's suitings. A pair of man's trousers that has become shiny can be cut up and made

[1] See p. 41.

into a skirt for yourself. Unpick the seams at the inside of the legs, open the material out, sponge away any stains, and press it. Then place your skirt pattern so that the waist part falls towards the trouser turn-up (the narrow part in both cases), and the fullness at the hem is provided for by the top waist of the trousers.

USEFUL AND BECOMING : THE PINAFORE FROCK

If you are the type of person who loves to wear jumpers and blouses but never feels happy in a skirt, cut up one of your older frocks into a pinafore dress.

To do this, cut the back of the bodice and the sleeves right out of the frock. When you are cutting off the bodice at the back, cut a good inch above the waist seam-line. This raw edge is then turned under double and hemmed flat along the back of the waist-line.

For the front of the dress, cut out of a piece of newspaper a heart-shaped pattern from 7 to 8 inches deep. When you have got this even each side, fold it in half and lay the bottom point of the heart on the lowest point of the centre-front of the bodice of the dress so that the full curve of the heart-shape lies on the side-seam. The top curve of the heart should be about 7 inches from the waist-line of the dress. Begin cutting at the top-centre point of the heart and cut round the side-seam down to a point 4 inches from the waist-line. Then turn the pattern right over and cut round it for the other side in the same way. This gives you a bib heart-shaped at the top, which is more becoming than the square type of bib.

From the back bodice make two long strips from 2 to 3 inches wide and 26 inches long. Turn them under and hem, and attach at each end, slightly slantwise, to either side of the bib at the top of the shaped part. Then, on the other ends, make a couple of loop buttonholes. The straps are taken from the front of your bodice over the shoulders, crossed over at the back, and fastened on to two small buttons, which should be sewn just inside the skirt waist at the back with about 10 inches between them. To make loop buttonholes, make a long, loose stitch about half-an-inch wide in the material, then make three more loose stitches of the same length in exactly the same place, so that you have four threads loose and of even length. Take one or two small back-stitches in the material to prevent the threads pulling tighter, and then work over them with buttonhole-stitch till they are completely covered.

If you have enough material in the back of the bodice, the shoulder-straps are best made double. If not, make several rows of close machine-stitching at the edges to strengthen them and keep them lying flat.

APRONS FROM OLD COTTON FROCKS

Never throw away faded or torn cotton frocks, and rather than tear them up for dusters, make yourself house-aprons with them. You can get two aprons from every frock.

Cut out the sleeves, then from the lower arm-hole cut straight across the top. The side-seams should be cut open, then hemmed down flat again. The back and front bodices are hemmed into square bibs. A couple of yards of ribbon, or coloured tape to attach to the bib of each apron, taken back over the shoulders, crossed over at the back, and brought round to tie at the waist-front will complete the garment.

AN OLD SHIRT MAKES A LOVELY BLOUSE

Few things are smarter on a woman than a blouse made of men's shirting, so don't tear up your husband's old shirts when they fray irreparably at the cuffs and neck, or split at the sides of the neck. Use the tails, which are nearly always in good condition, to make yourself a blouse. Use the basic bodice and sleeve pattern,[1] but be careful to place the sleeve pattern so that the stripes in the shirting are running *down* from the shoulder-line and not across. Unless, of course, you prefer to make your entire blouse up with the stripes running horizontally. In this case the bodice patterns are placed on the tails of the shirt at right angles to the neck, and you must be careful to lay the bottom of the back bodice, and the bottom of the front bodice, perfectly level along one of the stripes. This will ensure that when you come to join the blouse together the stripes will meet all round instead of being one just below the other.

CUTTING DOWN FOR THE CHILDREN

DELIGHTFUL summer frocks can be made for the four- to five-year-old girl from a shirt that has a blue and white or pink and white stripe. Darker stripes look rather too heavy on a young child, but a little frock in pastel stripes and bound with rick-rack braid (which costs a few pence a yard), or with cherry-coloured or royal blue tape, is charming.

If you are cutting down clothes for a younger child from those of an older one, or cutting down from your own or your husband's clothes, do have the patience to unpick the garment and entirely re-make it for the child. Children do so love to have something new that is completely their own, and it is really hardly any more trouble to remake for a child than to take in and fit and re-fit the same model so that it comes out looking just the same only a size smaller.

[1] See pp. 22 and 39.

Cut round the seams of grown-up garments, then steam and press all the pieces. Take the child's measurements, and then measure up on the pieces so that you know where you are going to be short of material, or where a shabby patch is going to be likely to show. Adjust the pattern you are using accordingly. A dark, plain skirt of your own can be transformed into a frock for your little girl. Give it something new to attract the child, a wool-embroidered yoke, or a dainty set of collar and cuffs made from the good part of one of your own fragile undergarments that is too torn to mend any longer.

WHAT TO DO WITH MEN'S CLOTHES

As MEN's clothes, when they become shabby, are almost impossible to re-make at home, they should be constantly kept in a state of good repair so that they will last longer.

Shirts are usually the main problem, as they fray at the cuff edges, and also split just below the neck-line where the waistcoat rubs them. As the cuffs of men's shirts are always made double, these can be " turned." To turn a cuff, unpick it carefully at the wrist-edge with a needle and a pair of small, sharp scissors to pull the stitches away. Take great care not to cut the material. When you have detached the cuff from the main garment, seam it along close to the edge just below the frayed part, then turn it inside out so that the frayed edge is now inside, and press it. Attach the cuff once more to the wrist-band by neatly hemming down either side, taking care to keep the gathers or pleats in the same position.

A PATCH FOR THE NECK OF A SHIRT

The split at the top of the shirt will have to be patched, but in such a way that it does not show. This means the patch must be large enough to come below the rim of the waistcoat at the bottom, and be level with the shoulder seam at the top. You will have to cut a piece from the tail of the shirt, and see that you cut it *up* from the tail and not lengthwise *across*, otherwise you'll have the stripes of the patch running in the wrong direction.

Pin on the patch, with the edges turned under, on the *right* side of the shirt, and with the top lying immediately under the shoulder-seam. Turn under the side edges so that stripe meets stripe. Then sew down, still on the right side, with small hemming-stitches. The material underneath should not be cut away, but lightly oversewn to prevent the edges from fraying. If it is not too badly split, but is torn in one rather narrow straight line, pull the edges together with fish-bone stitch. The hole you have left in the tail of the shirt should be filled in with a piece of cotton or another piece from an older shirt.

TO WASH AND IRON A MAN'S TIE

When you are ironing the creases out of a man's tie, place it between two layers of material—a piece of undressed muslin or cotton—and have the top one slightly damp and the bottom piece quite dry. Press with a fairly cool iron. If you are going to wash ties, remember to tack them securely along the edges first so that the interlining does not pull out. Never rub or stretch ties when you are washing them, rather knead them carefully with the fingers, and pull gently into shape before hanging up to dry.

A TIP ON MAKING MEN'S UNDERWEAR LAST

Men's and boys' underclothes should all be carefully patched when they begin to wear thin, and long before the holes arrive. If you are putting a patch on flannel, never turn under the inner edges of the worn part, but feather-stitch these edges flat to the main garment so that the patch is not bulky.

Much tearing and pulling of underpants, trousers and pyjamas is avoided if you strengthen the cross-seams at the crutch with pieces of tape. Sew the tape over the seams, hemming it down neatly each side, right across where the seams meet, and about an inch and a half along. It takes very little time to do this, and saves a great tear later on as the tape will take a lot of the strain from the main body of the garment.

TO CUT DOWN PYJAMAS FOR A SMALL BOY

If you are re-making men's pyjamas for a small boy, be careful to see that you are not using again the pieces that are already worn. The seat of a pair of pyjamas usually wears rather thin, so when cutting down for a child, use the man's coat to make the trousers for the child, and the lower part of the trouser-legs for the child's coat. In this way you even up the wear and tear on the fabric.

A NEW USE FOR DRESS SHIRTS

Never turn dress shirts into dusters. This fine linen is so very soft that it makes lovely hankies for all the family, both for ordinary times and when they have colds. Cut up and hemmed into large squares, they are excellent for use in the case of colds as they are so soft, and also they are not as bulky as the ordinary inexpensive handkerchief linen. For yourself, cut these shirts up into smaller squares and hem neatly or, if you prefer, whip on very narrow baby-lace edgings.

NEW COLOURS FOR OLD CLOTHES

IF ALL your clothes are good, mended, and of still wearable cut, but in colours that you now no longer care for, try dyeing them.

Dye only garments that are still good, as dyes weaken the fabric, and it is little use trying to dye an already much-worn garment if it is thin in places.

EQUIPMENT FOR DYEING

To dye at home you need 2 large basins (1 enamel), two long clean sticks to move your garment about in the basin, and a little bag to hold the dye, if it is a powder dye. A little bag made out of an odd scrap of muslin would do splendidly, or the foot of an old silk stocking. It is wise to wear rubber gloves or you will get the dye in your nails and find difficulty in removing it. Old towels or sheeting should be spread out on a flat surface first covered with newspaper, so that when you lay the garment you are dyeing out to dry, you do not dye most of your bathroom or kitchen with it.

The important thing about dyeing is to follow the instructions on the packet concerning how much water to mix with it, and so on. One packet of dye (sixpenny size) will dye about two yards of fabric, so make a rough estimate first of how much yardage there is in the garment you are going to dye.

STUDY THE COLOUR CHART FIRST

Also, before you start, make up your mind about the colour. Remember that the resulting colour will be the result of the dye itself, coupled with the original shade of the garment. Read the directions on the packet about this. You can't dye a red garment yellow, but if you attempt it you may get quite a reasonable shade of burnt orange.

HOW MUCH WATER DO I NEED?

Enough water must be used to immerse the garment completely. This is most important. Unless the whole garment is well under water the results will be patchy. All stains or grease spots on the garment should be removed before the dyeing process is begun. Weigh your garment on the kitchen scales, as the weight of it is what decides the amount of water to be used so that it is completely immersed. About ten times the weight of the material in water is the usual rule.

Mix your dye and then thoroughly damp the garment by putting it in a basin of tepid water. Don't put it into the dye wringing wet but when it is of an even dampness all over. Then when the dye is completely dissolved lower the garment into the basin. Stir it up all the time with the sticks, lifting and lowering and separating the material so that the dye has a chance to sink evenly into it all over. Here are a few facts concerning the reactions of various materials to dyes, and how to deal with them in detail.

TO CHOOSE THE RIGHT TEMPERATURE

Woollen fabrics should be plunged into the dyeing water when it is at a temperature of about 122 degrees Fahrenheit. Bring it to the boil, and then keep it simmering at the temperature indicated on the packet. These directions will also give you the length of time necessary for various types of garment.

Cotton fabrics, which absorb dye more slowly than woollen ones as they are more closely woven, can be put into a much stronger solution of dye, and into much hotter water. Silk should be boiled in a dye of medium strength, while rayon should only be put in a very weak solution, and never, never brought to the boil. In fact, it is a good rule to keep the dye for rayon at normal blood heat—a temperature into which you can put your hand and not draw it quickly out again.

TO RINSE DYED GARMENTS

When it comes to rinsing, lift the whole garment out carefully on your hands, with the aid of one of your mixing sticks if necessary, and plunge it immediately into the rinsing basin. Silks, cottons and rayons can be left in the rinsing water until it is cold, but wool should be put into the exact temperature of the dyeing basin water when you come to rinse it. Knead and pat as much moisture as you can from wool before you put it into the rinsing water, and fan the garment until it has ceased to steam. When you are rinsing dyed garments, don't pull them about or twist them, but lift them gently up and down on the hands to remove traces of the dye, squeezing it carefully with the knuckles against the sides of the basin, but not on any account *wringing* it.

Dark woollen garments should be put into a solution of gelatine to restore their stiffness, and cottons and muslins lightly starched.

Leave to dry, and then in all cases iron only on the *wrong* side. Cotton and silk should be ironed while they are still fairly damp.

Once you have dyed a garment, remember that if you ever should wish to iron it on the right side, you should always do so over a damp cloth, otherwise you are likely to get rather a horrid patchy result.

COLD WATER DYEING

Underclothes can often be given a freshened-up look by re-tinting, and this is best done with cold water dyes. These are only really suitable for thin fabrics as they are very delicate, are likely to fade sometimes, and ultimately come out with constant laundering.

To dye with a cold water dye, the dye is dissolved on the same principle as a shampoo, in a little hot water, strained into a basin through a piece of muslin, and cold water added until the desired depth of colour is acquired. The garment is then dipped in, swished round for a minute or two, then rinsed, dried and ironed in the same way as a garment dyed in hot water.

Lace, stockings, and white silk underwear can be tinted with tea or coffee in the same way. Undies of pale colours can also be dyed with coloured inks, but this is not really advisable as the chemicals in the ink in time rot the material. Remember that no kind of tinsel thread such as lamé or brocade will take dye, so don't try it.

If you wish to dye a garment black (such as a heavy coat), you would be well advised to have this done professionally. Black is the most difficult of all dyes to " take," and besides this you may not have the equipment necessary for dyeing such a large garment at home.

DRESSING THE CHILDREN

IT TAKES so little time, so little material to make children's clothes that this side of dressmaking is perhaps the most pleasurable of all. Children's fashions change very little, too, so that what you learn about making clothes for your first child will stand you in good stead for your whole family.

Dressmaking for children begins, of course, with the layette. In a simple layette that includes everything baby will need, there should be :

4 day gowns.	2 wool coatees, or matinée jackets.
3 flannel binders.	
3 silk and wool vests.	3 pairs woollen bootees.
3 long soft wool or fine flannel petticoats.	4 pilches.
	2 doz. gauze squares.
4 nightdresses (fine cotton or cambric).	2 doz. squares of Terry towelling.
6 bibs.	1 woollen shawl.
2 woollen bonnets.	3 pairs gloves.

Binders should be made from soft white cotton flannel. A quarter-of-a-yard of 36-inch material will make two binders. They should be about 6 inches deep and about 18 inches long.

The little vests should be knitted in silk and wool. Choose an easy straight-down pattern with ribbon threaded through the neck.

Petticoats are easily made from a pattern you can cut yourself. Remember, the simpler the garments the easier they will be to wash and iron. Never put pins into a baby's clothes, and never use buttons for fastenings, as the baby is liable to pull them off and swallow them.

PATTERN FOR A BABY'S PETTICOAT

To cut a pattern for the petticoats, cut a rectangle of newspaper 22 inches long by 11 inches wide. Measure from the top left-hand corner 2 inches in and an inch down, and cut out a small neck-curve between these two points. Then from the top neck point measure 2½ inches along and, from here, an inch-and-a-half down. Draw a line between these two points and cut along it for the shoulder. Measure 4 inches down from the front of the neck, and from this point draw a straight line across the rectangle and 6½ inches long. Between this point and

76

the end of the shoulder-seam, the arm-hole curve is cut. Then from the lower edge of the arm-hole draw a diagonal line across to the right-hand bottom corner of the rectangle, and cut along it. The bottom edge of the petticoat is now perfectly straight, but to make the garment hang properly round it off in a slight curve at the bottom right-hand edge—about an inch off the edge is enough.

This foundation pattern can also be used to make the day gowns and the nightdresses. The same pattern is used for the back and front of the gown, the neck being cut a little smaller at the back. For a petticoat of this type you need a yard-and-a-half of material. Remember, when cutting out the material, that no allowance has been left for turnings.

Make these petticoats from very fine flannel, or from nainsook, cambric or fine cotton. If you are using a cotton material, the seams should be seamed and felled, but if you are working on flannel, run and herring-bone the seams. The garment is opened by a cut down the centre-back about 10 inches long. Pierce little eyelet holes down the opening and lace through narrow ribbon. Bind the neck, arm-holes and hem of the petticoat with narrow ribbon or bias binding.

A COMFORTABLE NIGHTDRESS FOR BABY

Baby's nightdresses can be made from the same pattern, but these need sleeves. To make the pattern for the nightdress sleeve, cut a rectangle of paper $7\frac{1}{2}$ inches deep by $4\frac{1}{2}$ inches wide. From the top right-hand corner measure $2\frac{1}{4}$ inches to the left at the top and mark this point. Then again from the top left-hand corner measure $1\frac{1}{2}$ inches down. Draw a curve between these two points and cut along it. At the bottom left-hand corner measure in 1 inch and, from here, half-an-inch up. Draw a line from the $1\frac{1}{2}$-inch mark at the top to meet this point, and cut. Then cut in a very shallow curve to the bottom right-hand corner. This pattern is for half a sleeve, so when cutting the material cut on a double thickness.

Nightdresses must be warm, so make these of fine wincey, nun's veiling, or delaine. The neck of the nightdress should be slightly gathered and set into a band about 8 inches long. Gather the tops of the sleeves, and put the sleeves into the arm-holes so that the sleeve-seam is directly meeting the side-seam.

To gather up the fullness round the waist of the nightdress, make two slots about an inch wide and about 7 inches from the top, on either side of the nightie. Draw a length of ribbon through these two slots and tie behind. To trim the nightdress, use chain-stitch or feather-stitching round the neck, hem and wrists.

The day dresses are cut from the same pattern as the night-dress and petticoat, but these are made from fine muslin, cambric or nainsook. On these, which are made up in the same way as the nightdresses, you may like to use lace or embroidery for the wrists, neck and hem. Many lovely trimmings are available for baby clothes, and each mother will choose her own according to her personal tastes in the matter.

A DAINTY MATINÉE JACKET

You now need a pattern for baby's matinée jacket. Cut a rectangle of paper 12 inches long by 10 inches wide. At the top left-hand corner of the rectangle measure 2 inches along and 1 inch down. At the bottom left-hand corner measure 2 inches along. The top marks make the little neck curve, and an inward slanting line is drawn from the point marked 1 inch down from the top, to the point marked 2 inches in at the bottom. This makes the centre front line of the jacket.

To cut the sleeve, measure in 1 inch at the top right-hand corner, and measure down $4\frac{1}{2}$ inches. The sleeve is cut between these two points on a slightly outward curving line. Then measure up 2 inches from the bottom right-hand corner and, from here, 1 inch in. Cut from the bottom of the sleeve edge down to the point 1 inch in, making first a fairly deep curve for the underarm, and then merging the line into a slant for the side-seam. The bottom of the jacket pattern is rounded off to meet the point 1 inch in, where the side-seam ends.

These little jackets may be made of corded silk pique, of muslin, crêpe-de-chine, or of nun's veiling or fine flannel for winter wear.

CLOTHES FOR GROWING CHILDREN

WHEN you are making clothes for children, remember that they will grow out of them very fast, so make them with good turnings and with deep hems, and use trimmings like tucks and pleats so that you can let them out as the child grows.

Except for best wear, it is usually a waste of time to put a lot of embroidery work or intricate fine sewing into children's clothes, as they don't often take care of them, and the children themselves will feel much happier in simple garments that won't easily spoil.

HINTS ON CHOOSING CLOTHES

Buttons, which are easily pulled off by children, should always be sewn on a double thickness of material, or backed with a small square of matching material. Choose fabrics that will stand up to hard wear. For winter, serge, face-cloth, rep, and branded woollens made specially in narrow widths for children's wear are the best choice. For summer, choose fabrics that will wash well and easily, like rayon, cotton, muslin, lawn and voile. When you are making summer frocks for a little girl, always sew an odd piece of material into the waist of the frock so that it gets washed every time the frock is washed, and provides a piece of material for patching the same colour as the frock itself. Even the fastest of fast colours seem to wilt when worn by children.

See that the children's clothes are roomy. They should never be tight round the neck, arm-holes, or between the legs. Magyar shapes, or frocks that fall straight from a yoke, are the most comfortable for young children to wear.

Small boys up to the age of six or seven can be dressed in short trousers and jerseys, or short trousers and short-sleeved shirt-blouses. When making a shirt-blouse for a boy, remember that the fastenings should be put on the opposite side to those on girls' clothes, that is, buttons on the right and buttonholes on the left at the front of the shirt. This applies to coats, jackets, trouser flies and pyjamas.

In the case of very little boys, say up to four years old, knickers can be made at home in fine woollen, silk or linen material from a good pattern. I do not, however, advise mothers to make knickers for older boys when heavy tweed or suitings are required. The results are rarely satisfactory, and expose the child to laughter and teasing from his companions because of his " home-made trousers."

Children's clothes should always have pockets in them to enable the children to carry about their own odd bits and pieces, and their handkerchiefs.

If you are making frocks for your little girl, make knickers in the same fabric, and if it is dark wool, make linings for them of fine cambric or nainsook.

Rompers are excellent wear for children up to six. They give the child plenty of room to move about, are easy to wash, and look neat. For the older child, both girls and boys, dungarees are now popular, and are an excellent garment to substitute when the romper stage is over. Woollen jerseys or shirt blouses can be worn under dungarees.

AN OUTFIT FOR THE " UNDER-SIXES "

For outdoor wear, children up to six look best dressed in a coat cut on simple princess lines, a hat with a five-gored crown and small turn-up brim, and leggings or gaiters. The outfit should all be made from the same material, and for winter a good tweed is excellent. Later in the year, use a fine face-cloth in royal blue, raspberry pink ; or, if the child is dark, deep cerise is attractive.

When making a coat for a child, the collar and front facings should be interlined with canvas to make them sufficiently stiff. The canvas is tacked to the wrong side of the coat, and the canvas collar to the wrong side of the fabric collar. The material facing is then tacked to the collar and coat fronts with the right sides together, and the outer edges stitched round. The turnings should be trimmed fairly close to the edges, then the facing is turned over to the wrong side and pressed. For a very small child it is not necessary to use canvas in the coat. A whole outfit for a child of four, including gaiters, takes $3\frac{1}{4}$ yards of 36-inch material, or in tweed $2\frac{1}{4}$ yards of 54-inch material.

CLOTHES FOR SUNNY DAYS

Children should always be allowed as much sun and air on their bodies as is possible, so when the weather is warm, dress them in sunsuits and playsuits that will expose their arms and shoulders and backs to the sun, but be careful to protect their heads and necks with shady hats.

You can make a playsuit for a child of seven to ten years from 2 yards of 36-inch material without a pattern. Choose for it easily washed gingham, seersucker (which needs no ironing), or some attractive cotton print.

Take the 2 yards of material, lay them on a flat surface, and in the middle of this 72-inch length, parallel with the selvedges, measure the width of the child's waist at the front. Put two pins in to mark this width. Then at either side of the width make four deep inverted pleats about 6 inches wide, machining them down from the top to a depth of 6 or 7 inches. At the ends of the length of the material turn under a good hem and slip-stitch down. Set into a double waist-band, and fasten down the side-back with four large buttons. Cut a square bib to fit the child's chest, and sew press-studs on to the bottom of it and on the inside waist-band at the front of the skirt so that it is detachable. Join shoulder-straps to the side-fronts of the bib, let them cross over at the back and fasten on to the waist-band of the skirt.

A BLOUSE FOR VERY HOT WEATHER

Sometimes the sun may be too hot for the child to wear this type of playsuit without protection on the back of the neck and upper arms. You can make a magyar Hungarian blouse in thin muslin or cotton from 1 yard of 36-inch material.

To make the blouse, first cut off a piece of material 20 inches wide. Then fold the two edges of the 20-inch width in so that they meet together in the centre. Measure 10½ inches down each side from the top and mark with pins. Then measure 6½ inches along the top each side from the centre of the piece of material. The top front of the blouse should now measure 13 inches. Cut a curved line for the arm-holes from the two edges of the 13-inch line to the point at the sides already marked 10½ inches down.

The sleeves are made by cutting two pieces of material 13 inches deep and 18 inches wide from the strip of material now left over. Fold each piece in half so that the width is 9 inches across and the two sides 13 inches. Then along the open-edge side cut a curve to fit the arm-hole of the body of the blouse by cutting in an inward slope 1 inch in at the top to about 2½ inches up from the bottom of the rectangle of material. These curves should be 10½ inches deep to fit the arm-hole. To make up the blouse, first join together the whole length of the back. Then join together the little pieces left at the bottom of the arm-holes on the sleeves, and seam the sleeves into the main body of the garment, arm-hole to arm-hole. The 8 inches left at the top of the sleeves forms part of the gathered-up neck-line. Turn down a small hem along the top of the neck and sleeves, and run a draw-thread of ribbon or cord through the neck to gather up and tie at the front. The bottom of the blouse can be threaded with elastic, and the sleeve edges either with elastic or a cord or ribbon to match the neck.

TO MAKE A SUN BONNET IN AN HOUR

Little girls always look charming in sun bonnets, and you can run one up in less than an hour, without a pattern.

You need half-a-yard of 36-inch material. Fold it in half and cut into two pieces 15 inches long and 18 inches wide. One is for the bonnet and the other for the lining. This will fit a child of nine ; for smaller children slightly smaller pieces are needed. Place the two pieces of material together, right side to right side, and tack all along three sides, leaving one side, 15 inches deep, open. Now fold in half and, from the left-hand corner at the open edges, cut out a 6-inch square. Open out the material again and round off the corners of the uncut side (18 inches) which forms the front of the bonnet. Now machine down all round (still leaving one side open), turn inside out, and press. Then join the side pieces to the flap which forms the back and gather slightly at the top to fit the child's head.

To give extra neck protection make a little frill at the back with the remaining pieces of material. To do this, cut a rectangle of material to fit on to the back of the bonnet, hem the lower edge, gather the top edge slightly, and sew it on the underside of the back of the bonnet. Sew strings at the sides to tie beneath the child's chin.

For everyday wear, berets are most suitable for children. When you make a coat or dress for a child, buy an extra half-yard to make a beret.[1]

Knitted gloves[2] for children are the most suitable as they slip on and off so easily that the child will have no difficulty in putting the gloves on. They are also much cheaper, if you knit them yourself, than fabric or leather gloves which have to be bought.

THE SCHOOLGIRL'S WARDROBE

SIMPLICITY should be the keynote for the schoolgirl. The most important item in her wardrobe is, of course, her school uniform, usually a gym-slip and blouse. It is also usually the most expensive, while being at the same time indispensable. If, for the sake of economy, you decide to make it yourself, remember there are certain very definite rules which must be followed if the child's schooldays are not to be made miserable by wearing incorrect or ill-fitting uniform. In any case, you should find out from the school if there are any special regulations about gym-slips before you either buy or make one.

If you decide to make one, first buy a really good pattern. Do not attempt to cut out either a new gym-slip or a gym-blouse from an old one. It may look simple but it definitely is *not*.

Usually, schools like children to wear knickers to match the slip, and even if there is no rule about this it is a good economy measure.

A gym-slip and knickers to match take $2\frac{1}{8}$ yards of 54-inch material for a little girl 7-8 years old, while $2\frac{7}{8}$ yards are needed for a 14-year-old.

FAULTS TO AVOID IN A GYM-SLIP

The special points to remember when making up the slip are to get the skirt to hang without drooping anywhere, to make it the correct length, and to make the correct number of box-pleats in the right places.

When you have carefully followed all the instructions given with the pattern, and got as far as tacking the slip together, pay special attention to the hang of the skirt. To prevent it dropping at the sides, sew the shoulder-seams last, and take up more material at the outside edges of these seams than you do at the inside edges. The slip should have a hem at least 4 inches deep, and the final length should be about 2 inches above the

[1] See p. 89.   [2] See p. 103.

child's knee, unless there are school regulations to the contrary

Take great care to get the box-pleats at the back level with the front ones. To do this, lay the material on a flat surface, and pin in the back pleats first, then make the front pleats to lie directly over them. The yoke should not be attached to the skirt part of the slip until you have made sure the pleats are absolutely level. To keep the pleats from coming out in wear, the sides of them can be machine-stitched in a straight line very close to the edge part of the way down. This edge-stitching will prevent the pleats from coming out and save you a lot of pressing. It must, however, be quite even, and it is as well to draw a line straight down close to the outside edge of each pleat with a ruler and tailor's chalk, and then to machine along the line. To save the blouses worn under the tunic from rubbing against the serge yoke and wearing into a hole, bind the inside edge of the front yoke all round with a strip of silk or velvet 3 inches wide. There is then less friction when the lighter material of the blouse rubs against the yoke.

A CHILD'S GYM-BLOUSE

A child's gym-blouse takes 1⅝ yards of 36-inch material for a girl of 7 to 8 years old, and 1⅞ yards for a girl 13-14 years old.

The blouse is made up along the same lines as you would make a blouse for yourself, but particular care must be taken to get the set of the collar accurate, as the child will often be wearing a tie or her hockey colours under the collar and knotted in front, so that, unless the collar fits properly, it will bunch up or stick out at the front points.

The long piece down the front, in which the buttonholes are made to fasten the blouse, should be put on and properly finished off before the collar is attached. The collar should then be put on so that it lies flat on either side of this piece (usually about 1½ inches wide) and does not meet closely at the front as for an adult blouse. The space left at the front leaves room for the child's tie and will prevent the front of the collar from cockling.

GIVING A CHILD DRESS SENSE

Keep the rest of the schoolgirl's wardrobe as simple as possible, while paying special attention to the colours that suit her, and encouraging her to develop a dress sense by asking for her opinions and preferences and discussing them with her. Often the temptation is to dress the child up if she is a girl, and then worry her to death to keep her clothes clean and her " bits and bobs " in place. If she is fair, choose frocks of navy, of lighter blue for best, and of dusty pinks, all made very plainly with wool embroidery as trimming in preference to detachable collars and cuffs. A dark child looks well in nigger brown, green, and the orange shades of red. Silk and wool combinations should be worn next the skin, and over these a little bodice, then knickers to match the frocks. All clothes should be fairly loosely made.

A girl that has grown too fast and begins to look gawky can be helped over this awkward stage if she has her clothes chosen to minimise these faults. Dress her in pleated skirts, or a flared skirt and blouse, and over it a finger-tip length, loose, boxy jacket. It will help her figure and long legs and arms far more than a frock with a defined waist-line and tight sleeves.

IDEAS FOR HATS

Ask a woman what item of her wardrobe she has liked most within the last ten years and remembers best, and nine times out of ten the answer will be a hat. Hats provoke that dreamy look in the eye, that set of reminiscences that begins," When I was young . . ." or " When I first met Tom . . .", and ends with a lengthy description of a perfectly lovely hat.

At the other extreme is the woman who simply hates having to go to buy a hat because she can never find one to suit her. A hat should give you a feeling of well-being. You should feel prettier with your hat on than with it off, so when you go to choose one give yourself plenty of time, and make up your mind to enjoy it.

STUDY YOUR FIGURE WHEN CHOOSING HATS

Always see yourself in a full-length mirror in a new hat before you finally decide to buy it. It must be in keeping with the rest of the costume with which it is to be worn. Very high crowns on tall, thin women look ridiculous. A woman who is tall and thin should wear soft feminine toques, tricorns and bonnets, and if she is choosing a classic felt to wear with a tailor-made it should have a large brim to give her width.

Short, plump women should never wear large brims. They look like mushrooms in them. The *petite* woman can wear almost any hat except one with a large brim. On her the round, childish American felt with a turn-up brim all round is right for a tailored costume.

Halo hats usually give too much height to a long face but are perfect on the round and heart-shaped face.

HATS FOR THE SEASONS

Generally speaking, straws are worn with light-weight materials, felts and velours with heavy materials. If you are choosing a summer straw to wear with a very dressy, ornamented frock, don't choose one covered with flowers and veiling, or else you'll simply look overdressed. A fairly plain straw trimmed with ribbon is right. A simple frock that is draped and gathered can take a fussy hat. A tailored linen frock or summer suit should be crowned with a sailor straw or, if you are tall enough, a sombrero.

When you are choosing a winter hat look at it in relation to your coat. A brim that dips at the back is no good at all with a

high-collared overcoat, as the coat collar will knock it up over
your eyes. If you want a hat for a plain, tailored suit, get one
with simple lines. A hat with a small brim over the eyes and a
turn-up brim at the back is most suitable. Never buy a hat with
a very deep crown as this will date it.

MAKE YOUR HAT AND YOUR HAIR AGREE

Is your problem long hair and a bun? There is a right and
a wrong way of tackling this problem. The wrong way is to ask
for an extra large fitting and push your bun up into the back of
the hat. This not only leads to the extreme discomfort of hair-
pins jabbing into the back of your head, but in a week or two it
will pull the hat itself completely out of shape. The right way
is to choose a hat with either a turn-up brim at the back or a
very small one, dress your hair with the bun rather lower on
your neck, and leave it outside the hat. To balance the bun,
get a hat with a large flower at the front, bunched ribbon, or an
upright feather, so that the line of your head and the line of hat
complement each other.

All hats should be chosen with regard to the way you do your
hair. Fine hair which is apt to go wispy should never have a hat
that " perches " worn on it. Choose something that comes down
at the sides and has a brim or a veil at the back to hide straggling
ends. The coarser type of hair that stays set and tidy all the
time will look well under these " off the face " and " on top of
the head " hats.

NEW HATS FROM OLD

ARE you clever with your fingers? Have you ever thought of
altering a hat of which you have become tired, making it into
a different shape, or even of making an entirely new hat for
yourself?

Much can be done at home with hats which are of good
material but which may have lost their shape, shrunk in the rain
and become too small, or stretched and become too big. A felt
hat that has shrunk in the rain can be stretched by steaming it
and pulling it out to the required size at the same time.

Take out any lining there may be in the hat, and remove the
ribbon or trimmings. Then half fill a kettle with water, and
when it is boiling fast hold the hat in the steam, your fingers
inside the crown, and stretch it round with your hands.

TO TIGHTEN A HAT THAT HAS STRETCHED

To tighten a felt hat that has stretched, without cutting the
brim from the crown, make vertical tucks in the crown from

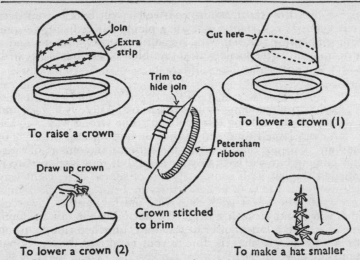

Join
Extra strip
To raise a crown
Cut here
To lower a crown (I)
Trim to hide join
Petersham ribbon
Draw up crown
Crown stitched to brim
To lower a crown (2)
To make a hat smaller

11. *Hats can be brought up-to-date by raising or lowering the crowns in the ways shown here. A hat that is too large may be cut and laced together so that the lacing forms a smart trimming.*

where the brim and crown join to a height of about 2 inches.

Mark the lines where the tucks will come with a piece of chalk, and then tack the lines so that you keep them accurate. The tucks are made by pinching the felt between the thumb and finger, and worked with stab-stitch[1] and a double thread for strength. Finish off on the wrong side.

These tucks can be made at the back of the hat, and then covered with a ribbon right round the crown or, if it is a ribbonless hat, make the tucks on the left-hand side of the hat. If you make five tucks and graduate their length, they will look like a trimming. The centre tuck should be the tallest, and the others graduated to a lesser height. If you find that the tucks look clumsy when you have finished them, cover them with a small cockade of feathers.

If your felt is too stiff to manipulate, you will have to cut the brim from the crown of the hat, cut the crown out at the back to tighten it, then join the edges together as for a hedge tear, i.e. hold the edges firmly between your left thumb and forefinger and use fish bone stitch to draw them together.

To put the brim back on to the crown, steam it until it shrinks to fit the new curve of the crown. Then try it on, and fit the brim on the crown so that it is comfortable. Join together on the underside with fish-bone stitch, and bind with dark tape.

[1] See p. 115.

TO HEIGHTEN OR LOWER A CROWN

A hat with too deep a crown can be altered in the same way. Cut off the brim, then cut off a couple of inches round the crown of the hat. To refit the brim, hold it in the steam of a fast-boiling kettle, and either pull out with your fingers to stretch it, or else shrink to the required length to suit the new crown. Join as above.

To give a shallow crown greater depth, cut off the brim close to where it joins the crown, and then cut a strip of buckram the required depth.

Sew the crown to the buckram, and then the brim. The buckram can be covered with a width of ribbon to match the hat, or in the case of a straw hat with a wreath of tiny flowers twisted together.

NEW LIFE FOR A RAIN-SPOILT STRAW

If you have a straw hat that has " risen " in the rain so that it now looks like a dustman's hat and you can do nothing with it, put a new crown in. To do this, cut away the brim, leaving about an inch of the old crown above it. Then make a soft crown for your hat. Measure across the diameter of the remains of the old crown, and then cut from a piece of muslin, or a piece of double tulle, a circle a quarter-of-an-inch larger in diameter. Turning under the edges of the circle, slip-stitch it down on to the piece of crown you have left for the base. Buy two or three posies of small flowers from any chain-store, take them to pieces, and sew the flowers flat over the soft crown of the hat. If you use tulle, or a piece of fancy-patterned silk, use it double, and in these cases you will not need the extra trimming of flowers.

TO KEEP HATS LOOKING SPRUCE

Hats which look shabby can often be given a new lease of life if they are re-trimmed. All ribbons and linings of hats should be removed and washed and pressed regularly. Ribbons should be washed in soapy lukewarm water, rinsed in warm water to which you have added a little vinegar. If the ribbon loses its " body," dissolve a teaspoonful of ordinary gum in a pint of boiling water. Leave to cool, then soak the ribbon in it for a few minutes. Dry it between a soft towel, squeezing out the moisture with your hands, and roll into a tight roll. A corded or patterned ribbon is ironed on the wrong side; dark-coloured ribbons should also be ironed on the wrong side. Smooth-faced and pastel-coloured ribbons should be ironed on the right side.

TRIMMINGS TO TRANSFORM YOUR MILLINERY

When it comes to re-trimming your own hats watch the way fashion is going, and then pick up oddments from the haberdashery counters to smarten your own millinery. Large buttons or unusual buckles look very well threaded or sewn on to narrow ribbon and put on the front of a hat. The art of sewing trimmings on to hats is to do it inconspicuously. To do this, use tie-stitch. It is like stab-stitch in that the needle is brought through from the back of the hat, put in again over the trimming to secure it, with a small stitch, and then tied to the first end of cotton on the wrong side.

Three lengths of narrow ribbon in different colours to pick up the colours of your blouses or jumpers makes an effective trimming for a dark hat worn with a dark suit. If you have a pair of nice dress-clips, fasten them into the front of your hat occasionally.

EXPENSIVE-LOOKING POSIES FOR A FEW PENCE

If you like flower-trimmed hats, buy a few bunches of different-coloured flowers from a chain-store for a few pence. When you get them home, unwire them, and re-mix together in smaller bunches, then sew them in mixed very small posies round the crown of a hat. A bunch of violets, a bunch of tiny pink rose-buds, and a bunch of forget-me-nots can be re-sorted into small Victorian posies, and in this way are given a more expensive and delicate look than if you bought three bunches of violets and left it at that.

BRINGING A WAVY BRIM INTO LINE

The wavy brim of a good hat can be trimmed so that it will look like a new hat, and straighten the brim at the same time. Buy enough milliner's wire to go round the brim, and oversew it not too closely together, right round the brim. Pull the brim back into shape with your fingers, and then bind with a narrow corded ribbon in a contrasting colour, or in the case of a felt hat, with ribbon velvet.

HATS YOU CAN MAKE YOURSELF

BERETS are always in fashion, and few things are more becoming, as they are soft enough to pull into shape on the head to suit any face. This is the way to make a beret in one piece of material.

First of all you must take your head measurements by putting a tape-measure round your head where the beret is to fit, that is, round the top of the forehead, and meeting just above the nape of the neck. This gives you the fitting of the underside for the beret.

Cut out a circle about 10 inches in diameter, and then with tailor's chalk divide the circle up into eight equal parts. This is done by drawing a line with a ruler straight through the middle of the circle, from top to bottom, then another one crossing it from side to side. The circle is now divided into quarters ; bisect these so that they are in eighths.

At the far edge of the circle, and exactly on these eight points, make darts about 4 inches deep and 1 to $1\frac{1}{2}$ inches across. These darts shape the underside of the beret. Sew up the darts, then fit the edge of the underside into double binding cut to the length of the head measurement already taken.

A FISH-NET TOQUE

A very pretty toque can be made from 4 yards of coloured fish-net and $\frac{3}{4}$ yard of buckram. Cut the buckram 4 inches wide, and long enough to fit round your head, then join it up into an upstanding circle, by sewing the two ends together with stab-stitch.[1] Cut off half-a-yard of fish-net to make the crown of your hat, and wind the rest of it round the buckram shape. Leaving a length of about 10 inches to hang loose, start winding over and over the buckram from the back of the shape. Do this fairly tightly so that there are no gaps of buckram showing. When you have covered the shape, fold the fish-net into one-third of its width and wind round a second time so that you get an even, substantial roll all round the shape. The end left over is allowed to hang loose at the back with the end that you left when you started.

To make the crown, put the half-yard of fish-net loosely over your head, and fit the shape down on to it. When it is comfortable, lift it off carefully, holding the top piece for the crown in place as you do so. Then turn it upside down and carefully pin the crown into the shape all round. Sew down firmly and your toque is finished.

CLOTH HATS FOR YOURSELF AND THE CHILDREN

Now that there will soon be no more straw available, it is worth while to know how to make cloth hats from tweed, or any wool fabric heavy enough for this purpose. On this foundation also children's simple cloth or felt hats are made.

To do this, take your head measurements. Firstly, measure all round the head, over the top part of the forehead, and down to the nape of the neck. Then measure over the head from the point of the forehead in line with the nose to just over the crown at the back.

To make a pattern for the crown of the hat, cut a strip of paper the length of your all-round head measurements plus $1\frac{1}{2}$ inches. The width should be the measurement of the

[1] See p. 115.

distance between your forehead and a very little way down the back of your head. Divide the strip of paper equally into six parts, and make six darts about half-way up the strip to form the crown. Fit the edges together as neatly as you can, and cut away the surplus paper. Now join the strip of paper into a circle, and you can then get the sections for a tweed or cloth hat by cutting down to the bottom of each dart and thus providing a pattern for each separate piece. Children's hats are made on this principle, though four sections are usually enough for a child's hat.

To cut the brim, make a paper pattern from a circle, and cut out the middle of it. When making up a tweed hat, always stitch it together from the top of the crown towards the brim. To stiffen the brim, use French canvas between double material.

SERVICE AND FAMILY WOOLLIES

Many women who have never knitted before in their lives may begin to learn now, so they can knit warm clothing for their men in the Services, or save money by knitting clothes for their children. If you are one of those who come fresh to knitting, you will need to master these elementary steps before beginning on the patterns for garments, which are designed to appeal to both novice and expert.

Casting on.—Make a slip loop, and put it on to the left-hand needle. Knit a plain stitch into the loop by putting the point of the right-hand needle through the loop on the right-hand side. Now pass the wool over the point of the right-hand needle, and bring the point of the needle over the wool and back through the loop, bringing the wool with it as it comes, and putting the new loop thus made on to the left-hand needle. Continue thus till you have the required number of stitches.

To give a firm edge to a garment, knit into the back of each loop for the first row after casting on. If an elastic edge is required knit into the back of every other stitch.

Plain Knitting.—This is commonly known as garter-stitch and is done in the same way as casting on, except that as the new loops are drawn through they remain on the right-hand needle, and the old loop is slipped off the left-hand needle. When you are knitting on four needles, however, garter-stitch is made by knitting 1 row plain and 1 row purl.

Purl Knitting.—This is done by holding the needle with the stitches on it in your left hand, slipping the first stitch and bringing the wool forward between the points of the two needles. Then put the point of the right-hand needle through the front of the first loop (the side nearest you), and pass the wool round the point of the right-hand needle. Now draw the point back through the loop, leave the new stitch on the right-hand needle, and slip the old loop off the left-hand needle. The wool is now in front of the right-hand needle. Insert the point of the right-hand needle through the front of the next loop, pass over the wool, and knit and slip the stitch off as before.

Stocking-stitch.—Knit alternate rows of plain and purl when working on two needles, and all plain when working on four.

To Cast off.—Knit the first two stitches, and pass the first one over the second, and off the needle. Knit the next stitch and repeat until you have only one stitch left, then thread the end of the wool through this remaining stitch, pull it up tight, and darn it in along the edge.

To Cast off a Double Row of Stitches.—See that there are an equal number of stitches on both needles. Put the point of a third needle through the two first stitches on each needle and knit them together, then knit the next two together, and draw the first stitch on the right-hand needle over the second. Continue this until the whole row is cast off, and finish as for a single row of stitches by drawing the end of the wool through the last stitch.

Grafting.—Grafting is mostly used for joining seams such as shoulder-seams on a pullover, and also to cast off stitches at the toe of a sock or stocking.

To graft a stocking toe, have the right side of the toe towards you and break off the wool, leaving a loose end about 12 inches long. Thread the wool through a darning needle. Holding the

12. *Casting off by grafting the stitches together with a darning needle gives a smooth and ridgeless finish to a toe or a seam.*

knitting needles parallel, thread the darning needle through the first stitch of the front needle as if you were going to knit the stitch. Draw the thread through, but do not slip the stitch off the knitting needle. Then thread the darning needle purl-wise through the first stitch of the back needle and from back to front through the second stitch on the back needle. Leave both stitches on the knitting needle while you thread the darning needle through the front of the first stitch on the first needle and from back to front through the second stitch on the front needle. The first stitch on the front needle and on the back needle may now be slipped off the knitting needle, if desired, but the work will be equally satisfactory if all the stitches are retained on the knitting needles till the grafting is finished.

To continue, thread the wool through the second and third stitches on the back needle and then through the second and third stitches on the front needle, and proceed thus to the end. When the last stitches have been threaded, darn in the thread.

To Increase.—Increasing is best done at the beginning or

end of a row, and there are three ways of doing it. The first, which is the simplest, is to wind the wool once round the right-hand needle where the extra stitch is to come, and then continue knitting. The second way is to pick up one of the stitches from the row below the needle and knit into it. The third, and best way, is to knit a stitch, but before slipping it off the needle, knit into the back of the loop thus knitting twice into one stitch.

To DECREASE.—Decreasing, again, is best done at the beginning or end of a row. You may either knit two stitches together (or purl together when using purl-stitch) or slip one stitch, knit the next, and pass the slipped stitch over the knitted one, and slip it off the needle.

MOSS-STITCH.—Cast on an odd number of stitches.

1st row.—K1, p1. *2nd row.*—K1, p1. If you want a large pattern, k2, p2.

When knitting moss-stitch, always start the return row with k1 or 2, depending on whether the design is k1, p1, or k2, p2, if you finish with k1 or k2. If you finish with p1 or p2, start with p1 or p2.

To work moss-stitch on 4 needles, knit as follows :

1st round.—K1, p1, ending with p1. *2nd round.*—P1, k1, ending with p1. Rep. 1st and 2nd rounds alternately.

ABBREVIATIONS

The following abbreviations for stitches and processes are used throughout the patterns for knitted garments :

beg.	beginning.	rem.	remain, remaining.
dec.	decrease.	rep.	repeat.
in.	inch.	s.	slip.
inc.	increase.	st.	stitch.
k.	knit (i.e. knit plain)	sts.	stitches.
m.-s.	moss-stitch.	s.-st.	slip-stitch.
p.	purl.	tog.	together.
p.s.s.o.	pass slipped stitch over.	wl. fwd.	wool forward.
		st.-st.	stocking-stitch.

SERVICE GARMENTS

I AM giving you patterns here for the principal woollen garments that your friends or relatives in the Services will want to include in their kit. Most of the garments are suitable for Navy, Army and Air Force personnel, as well as for members of the Civil Defence Services, according to the colours in which you make them. And don't forget that the men at home who spend long, cold hours fire-watching or digging for victory will need pullovers, gloves and socks too. For them, of course, you can use any colour wool they fancy and that is procurable.

BALACLAVA HELMET

Materials.—2½ ozs. 4-ply fingering ; 4 No. 9 needles with double points ; 2 No. 7 needles.

Commence at lower edge by casting on 96 sts. fairly loosely on 3 No. 9 needles (32, 32, 32). Work in rounds of ribbing of k2, p2 for 5 ins. *Next round.*—K2, p2 6 times, and leave these 24 sts. on stitch-holder for face. Put all the remaining 72 sts. on to one of the No. 7 needles, and then work 60 rows in garter-stitch (every row knit). *Next row.*—K47, s1, k1, p.s.s.o., turn. *Next row.*—K23, s1, k1, p.s.s.o., turn. Rep. last row till 24 sts. remain.

Change to No. 9 needles and rib in k2, p2 over these 24 sts. Then pick up and rib in k2, p2 32 sts. down side of face, rib over 24 sts. on stitch-holder, pick up and rib 32 sts. up second side of face (112 sts.). Arrange these sts. on 3 needles (36, 40, 36) and rib in k2, p2 for 12 rounds. Cast off in rib.

CAP TO WEAR UNDER A STEEL HELMET

Materials.—1 oz. double knitting wool ; 4 No. 8 needles.

Measurements.—The cap should measure 7 inches from edge to crown. If you are a loose knitter, use No. 9 needles and knit 2 more rows than suggested below.

Cast on 72 sts. loosely. K2, p2 for 20 rows. K. for 19 rows. *20th row.*—K7, k2 tog. ; rep. for row. *21st row.*—K. *22nd row.*—K6, k2 tog ; rep. for row. *23rd row.*—K. *24th row.*—K2 tog. twice ; p1, p2 tog. twice ; k1 ; rep. for row. *25th row.*—K. *26th row.*—K2 tog. 3 times, p1 ; rep. for row. *27th row.*—K. *28th row.*—K2 tog. till 8 sts. rem., then sew or graft off.

A PAIR OF WARM GLOVES

Materials.—2½ ozs. 4-ply wool ; 4 No. 12 needles with double points.

Tension.—About 8 sts. and 11 rows to one inch.

RIGHT-HAND GLOVE.—Cast on 64 sts. on to 3 needles (20, 24, 20). Work in rounds of rib of k2, p2 for 3 ins.

Next round.—K1, inc., k3, inc., k. to end of round. Knit 3 rounds. *Next round.*—K1, inc., k5, inc., k. to end of round. Knit 3 rounds. *Next round.*—K1, inc., k7, inc., k. to end of round. Knit 3 rounds. *Next round.*—K1, inc., k9, inc., k. to end of round. Knit 3 rounds. *Next round.*—K1, inc., k11, inc., k. to end of round. Knit 3 rounds. *Next round.*—K1, inc., k13, inc., k. to end of round. Knit 3 rounds. *Next round.*—K1, inc., k15, inc., k. to end of round. Knit 3 rounds. *Next round.*—K1, inc., k17, inc., k. to end of round. *Next round.*—K2, slip next 19 sts. on piece of wool for thumb, cast on 3, k. to end of round (20, 24, 20). Knit in plain rounds for 1½ ins. Divide for fingers as follows :

1st FINGER.—K9, slip all but the last 9 sts. on piece of wool, cast on 2, k. last 9 sts. (20 sts.). Arrange on 3 needles and knit in plain rounds for 3 ins. *Next round.*—Dec., k2, 5 times. *Next round.*—K. *Next round.*—Dec., k1, 5 times. *Next round.*—Dec. all round. Break off wool, leaving long end. Thread wool through darning needle, draw up sts. tightly, and fasten off.

2ND FINGER.—K. next 8 sts. from piece of wool, cast on 2, k. the last 8 sts. from wool, pick up 2 cast-on sts. of previous finger (20 sts.). Arrange on 3 needles and k. in plain rounds for 3¼ ins. Complete as for 1st finger. Fasten off securely.

3RD FINGER.—Work exactly as for 2nd finger, but till 3rd finger is only 3 ins. long.

4TH FINGER.—Pick up rem. 14 sts. and pick up 2 cast-on sts. of previous finger. Arrange on 3 needles and k. in plain rounds for 2¼ ins.

Next round.—Dec., k2, 4 times. *Next round.*—K. *Next round.*— Dec., k1, 4 times. Fasten off as for 1st finger.

THE THUMB.—Pick up 19 sts. from wool and pick up 3 cast-on sts. Arrange these 22 sts. on 3 needles and k. in plain rounds for 2¾ ins.

Next round.—K2, dec., k2, 5 times. *Next round.*—K. *Next round.* —K2 tog., then dec., k1, 5 times. Fasten off as for 1st finger.

LEFT-HAND GLOVE.—Work as for right-hand glove until 1st finger is reached.

1ST FINGER.—K. the first 16 sts., slip all but the last 2 sts. on piece of wool, cast on 2, k. last 2 sts. (20 sts.). Arrange on 3 needles and k. in plain rounds for 3 ins. Complete this finger and rem. of glove as for right-hand glove.

MITTENS WITH FINGERS

Materials.—3 ozs. double knitting wool ; 4 No. 9 needles with pointed ends.

Commence at wrist, casting on 44 sts. on 3 needles (16, 12, 16). Join in a round and work in rounds of rib of k2, p2 for 3½ ins. *Next 3 rounds.*—K. *Next round.*—K1, inc., k. till 2 rem,. inc., k1. *Next round.*—K. *Next round.*—K2, inc., k. till 3 rem., inc., k2. *Next round.*—K. *Next round.*—K3, inc., k. till 4 rem., inc., k3. *Next round.*—K. *Next round.*—K4, inc., k. till 5 rem., inc., k4. *Next round.*—K. *Next round.*—K5, inc., k. till 6 rem., inc., k5. *Next round.*—K. *Next round.*—K6, inc., k. till 7 rem., inc., k6. *Next round.*—K. *Next round.*—K7, inc., k. till 8 rem., inc., k7. *Next 5 rounds.*—K. *Next round.*—K. till 8 rem., slip these remaining sts. and the first 8 sts. from the first needle on to a piece of wool and leave for thumb. Now cast on 2 sts., and put one of these sts. at end of 3rd needle and one at beginning of 1st needle (16, 12, 16). *Next 13 rounds.*—K.

Divide for fingers as follows :

1ST FINGER.—K7, slip all but the last 7 sts. on a piece of wool, cast on 2, k7 (16 sts.). Arrange on 3 needles, k. one round plain, then k. in rib of k1, p1 for 3 rounds. Cast off in rib.

2ND FINGER.—Pick up and k. next 5 sts. from piece of wool, cast on 2, pick up and k. last 5 sts. from piece of wool, pick up 2 cast-on sts. of previous finger (14 sts.). Arrange on 3 needles k. one round, then rib in k1, p1 for 3 rounds. Cast off in rib.

3RD FINGER.—Work as for 2nd finger.

4TH FINGER.—Pick up and k. rem. 10 sts. and 2 cast-on sts. of previous finger (12 sts.). Work as for 2nd finger.

THUMB.—Pick up and k. 16 sts. from piece of wool and 4 sts. from base of thumb. Arrange on 3 needles, k. one round, then work in rib of k1, p1 for 3 rounds. Cast off in rib.

Make another mitten in same way. Press the mittens well with warm iron over a damp cloth.

LONG-SLEEVED, POLO-NECKED PULLOVER

This pullover pattern can be made in two sizes, and instructions are given for both. FIRST SIZE.—Shoulder to lower edge, 22 ins. ; round chest below arm-holes, 36 ins. ; sleeve-seam, 19 ins. SECOND SIZE.—Shoulder to lower edge, 24 ins. ; round chest below arm-holes, 38 ins. ; sleeve-seam, 20 ins.

Materials.—FIRST SIZE.—12 ozs. 4-ply fingering. SECOND SIZE.—14 ozs. 4-ply fingering. 2 No. 12 and 2 No. 9 knitting needles ; 4 No. 9 needles with pointed ends for collar.

Tension.—About 6½ sts. to 1 in.

To work the first size, follow the directions, omitting the instructions given in brackets. To work the second size, follow the directions as varied by the instructions in brackets.

BACK AND FRONT ALIKE.—Using No. 12 needles, commence at lower edge, casting on 116 sts. for first size (or 124 sts. for second size). K. in ribbing of k2, p2 for 3 ins. Change to No. 9 needles. K. in st.-st. till work measures 14½ ins. (or 16 ins. for second size) from lower edge, ending with a p. row.

To dec. for arm-holes, k. 12 rows st.-st., dec. 1 st. at beg. and end of every row. This leaves you 92 sts. (100 sts. for second size). K. in st.-st. till work measures 22 ins. (or 24 ins. for second size) from lower edge, ending with a p. row.

SHAPE NECK AND SHOULDERS AND DIVIDE FOR NECK.—For first size, cast off 6, k24, turn, p24. *Next row.*—Cast off 6, k18, turn, p18. *Next row.*—Cast off 6, k12, turn, p12. *Next row.*—Cast off 6, k6. Cast these 6 sts. off. Slip next 32 sts. on to a piece of wool for collar, join on wool. *Next row.*—K. *Next row.*—Cast off 6, p. to end. Rep. last 2 rows 3 times. Cast off. (For second size, cast off 7, k27, turn, p27. *Next row.*—Cast off 7, k20, turn, p20. *Next row.*—Cast off 7, k13, turn, p13. *Next row.*—Cast off 7, k6. Cast these 6 sts. off. Slip next 32 sts. on to a piece of wool for collar, join on wool. *Next row.*—K. *Next row.*—Cast off 7, p. to end. Rep. last 2 rows 3 times. Cast off.)

Rep. from the beg. for the back of the pullover.

THE SLEEVES (both alike).—Using No. 12 needles, commence at cuff, casting on 64 sts. K. in ribbing of k2, p2 for 3 ins. Change to No. 9 needles. K. in st.-st., inc. 1 st. at beg. and end of next and every 8th row till 92 sts. are on needle (or 98 sts. for second size). Continue to k. in st.-st. till sleeve measures 19 ins. (or 20 ins. for second size), ending with a p. row.

TO SHAPE TOP.—K. 40 rows st.-st., dec. 1 st. at beg. and end of every row, leaving 12 sts. (18 sts. for second size). Cast off.

THE COLLAR.—Using the 4 No. 9 needles, pick up 96 sts. round neck. Divide on to 3 needles (32, 32, 32). Join on wool and k. in rounds of ribbing of k2, p2 for 7 ins. Cast off loosely.

Sew up underarm and sleeve-seams. Sew in sleeves, placing sleeve-seam level with underarm. Press seams.

A PAIR OF THICK SOCKS

Materials.—6 ozs. 3-ply wool wheeling ; 4 No. 11 needles with points both ends.

Cast on 52 sts. (16, 20, 16). Work 4 ins. in rounds of k1, p1. Then work 2½ ins. in plain knitting. Dec. once at beg. of 1st and at end of 3rd needle, in the next and every 7th round until there are 46 sts. Continue without shaping until work measures 11 ins. from the beg.

TO SHAPE THE HEEL.—K. the first 13 sts. of the round on to one needle, slip the last 13 sts. of the round on to the other end of the same needle. (These 26 sts. form the heel.) Divide the rem. sts. on to two needles, and leave for instep.

TO WORK HEEL.—*1st row.*—S1, k1, k. to end of row. *2nd row.*—P. back. Rep. these two rows 18 times, always slipping the first st. of every k. row and knitting the last st. of every p. row.

TO TURN THE HEEL.—K15, s1, k1, p.s.s.o., k1, turn, p6, p2 tog., p1, turn, k7, s1, k1, p.s.s.o., k1, turn, p8, p2 tog., p1 ; continue as above till all sts. are on needle (16 sts. in all), ending with a k. row.

Now take another needle and k. up 16 sts. from side of heel ; with a second needle, k. the instep sts. ; with a third needle, k. up 16 sts. from the other side of heel, and 7 sts. from bottom of heel. Slip the remaining 7 sts. from bottom of the heel on to the first needle.

*K. two rounds of plain knitting. *3rd round.*—K. to the last 3 sts. of the first needle ; k2 tog., k1. Knit second needle plain. On third needle, k1, s1, k1, p.s.s.o., k. to end of round.* Rep. from * to * until first and third needles each have 13 sts.

Continue without shaping until the foot measures (from where the stitches were knitted up at the heel) : 6½ ins. for a 10-in. foot, 7 ins. for a 10½-in. foot, 7½ ins. for an 11-in. foot.

To Shape the Toe.—*1st round.*—K. to last 3 sts. of the first needle. K2 tog., k1. On the second needle, K1, s1, k1, p.s.s.o., k. to last 3 sts., k2 tog., k1. On the third needle, k1, s1, k1, p.s.s.o., k. to end of needle. *2nd round.*—K.

Rep. these two rounds till 16 sts. rem. K. the sts. of the third needle on to the end of the first needle, and graft.[1]

SPIRAL STOCKINGS FOR GUMBOOTS

Materials.—6 ozs. oiled wool ; 4 No. 8 needles, 4 No. 9 needles (both sets pointed at each end).

Measurements.—Total length, 24 ins. ; length of foot, 11 ins.

Cast on very loosely in double wool (for strength) 54 sts. (18, 18, 18) on No. 8 needles.

Break off 1 strand. Now rib in k1, p1 for 15 rows. K5, p1 for 5 rounds. *Next round.*—*Move p. st. one forward, and k5, p1. This pushes the p. st. one forward each time, and forms the spiral. Continue for 5 rounds.* Rep. from * to * till leg measures 12 ins. Change to No. 9 needles and k. 4 ins. more (16 ins.).

To Shape Foot.—Take 2 tog. at the p. st., thus making k4, p1 all round (45 sts.). Continue till total length is 24 ins.

The Toe.—This is all knitted plain. *1st round.*—Dec. every 5th st. all round. K. 4 rounds. *6th round.*—Dec. every 4th st. all round. K. 4 rounds. *11th round.*—Dec. every 3rd st. all round. K. 3 rounds. Draw wool through all sts., draw up and darn in the end very firmly, making a round toe.

A FIRST SET FOR BABY

War or peace, most mothers like to knit their babies' clothes themselves. They are very quickly done, and the making of them provides a restful occupation. The newly-arrived baby will be warm and comfortable in the garments for which patterns are given here. Only 10 ozs. of wool are needed to make two of each garment recommended.

A WOOLLY BONNET

Materials.—½ oz. 3-ply wool ; a pair of No. 8 needles ; 1½ yards of 1-inch ribbon.

[1] See p. 93.

Cast on 76 sts. and work 1½ ins. in plain knitting. Now work in st.-st., keeping 4 sts. in garter-stitch at each side, until the work measures 5½ ins.

Keeping a garter-stitch border at each side, k6, k2 tog. all along next row. *Next row.*—P. *Next row.*—K5, k2 tog. all along row. *Next row.*—P. *Next row.*—K4, k2 tog. all along row. *Next row.*—P. *Next row.*—K3, k2 tog. all along row. *Next row.*—P. Break off wool, leaving a long end, draw the wool through the sts., pull up and sew to shape.

Press bonnet, making a turn-over round face with the plain border. Divide ribbon into halves, and sew on to bonnet with rosettes at each side.

A PAIR OF BOOTEES

Materials.—½ oz. 3-ply wool ; a pair of No. 8 needles.

Cast on 34 sts. and k. 4 rows plain. Change to st.-st. and work until 3 ins. are completed, finishing at a p. row.

Next row.—K2,* make 1, k2 tog., k1. Rep. from *, ending k2. P. back.

Next row.—K11, then slip these sts. on to a safety-pin, k12, and put rem. 11 sts. on to another pin. P. back 12 sts.

Work 18 more rows in st.-st. on the centre 12 sts., finishing after a p. row.

Break off wool, then re-join wool and knit across 11 sts. from first safety-pin, pick up 13 sts. from side of centre piece, k. across centre 12 sts., then pick up 13 sts. down side and k. 11 sts. from other safety-pin (60 sts. on needle). P. back 60 sts.

Work 6 rows in st.-st.

Next row.—K2 tog., k26, k2 tog., k2 tog., k26, k2 tog. *Next row.*—P2 tog., p24, p2 tog. twice, p24, p2 tog. *Next row.*—K2 tog., k22, k2 tog. twice, k22, k2 tog. *Next row.*—P2 tog., p20, p2 tog. twice, p20, p2 tog. Cast off.

Press, sew up foot and leg seams, and thread a crochet cord or narrow ribbon through the row of holes.

PATTERN FOR A PAIR OF LONG LEGGINGS

Materials.—2 oz. 2-ply wool ; 4 No. 10 needles, pointed at both ends.

Measurements.—Length, 17½ ins.

With two needles, cast on 72 sts. Work in rib of k1, p1 for 2 ins.

To give fullness at back, k. 8 sts., turn and p. back, then k. 16 sts., turn and p. back, k. 24 sts., turn and p. back, k. 32 sts., turn and p. back, and continue knitting 8 sts. more each time until 16 sts. are left. K. one row right across, and leave.

Taking the other two knitting needles, cast on another 72 sts.

and rib in k1, p1 for 2 ins. P. 8 sts., turn and k. back, p. 16 sts., turn and k. back, and continue knitting 8 sts. more each time until 16 sts. rem. P. right across row.

Now divide the 144 sts. on to 3 needles (48 on each), seeing that the centre back is in the middle of the back needle, with 48 on each of the two side needles, the division coming at the centre-front. Knit plain in rounds until the work measures 7 ins. from commencement of ribbing.

THE GUSSET.—Starting at the back needle, k22, inc. by knitting twice into the next st., k1, inc. in the next st., k23. On the second needle, k46, inc. in the next st., k1. Inc. in the first st. of the third needle, then k47. K. 2 rounds plain.

Starting at the back needle, k22, inc. in the next st., k3, inc. in the next st., k23. On the second needle, k46, inc. in the next st., k2. On the third needle, k1, inc. in the next st., k47. K. 2 rounds plain.

Starting at the back needle, k22, inc. in the next st., k5, inc. in the next st., k23. On the second needle, k46, inc. in the next st., k3. On the third needle, k2, inc. in the next st., k47. K. 2 rounds plain.

Continue increasing every third round in this manner until there are 24 more sts. on the back and 24 more on the front (12 increasings altogether). Put 72 sts. from one side on to a stitch-holder for one leg, and graft the 24 sts. of the front and back gusset together. Proceed to work one leg on the rem. 72 sts., dividing the sts. on to 3 needles (24 on each). Join wool at the back needle next to gusset and k. one round plain.

Without decreasing on the back needle, but decreasing on each of the other two needles immediately after and immediately before the back needle every other round, continue working round in plain knitting until there remain 12 sts. on each of the two side needles and until the leg measures 3 ins.

THE ANKLE.—First work 2 ins. in rib of k1, p1. Then, working 1 row plain, dec. 1 st. at beg. and end of the back needle, dec. 1 at the beg. of the second needle, and dec. 1 at the end of the third needle. K. plain without decreasing for 1½ ins.

THE TOE.—Dec. by knitting 2 tog. at the beg. and end of the back needle, 2 tog. at the beg. of the second needle, and 2 tog. at the end of the third needle. Dec. in this way on each round until there are 10 sts. on the back needle and 5 on each of the other two. Put the two sets of 5 sts. on to one needle, then graft the two sets of 10 sts. tog.

Pick up the sts. left on the wool-holder and k. the second leg to match.

Sew waist ribbing together at the back, leaving opening at

the front. Press, and thread ribbon round waist, leaving sufficient ends to tie in a bow at the front.

FINGERLESS MITTENS

Materials.—½ oz. 3-ply wool ; 1 pair No. 11 knitting needles ; ¾ yard baby ribbon.

Cast on 54 sts., and work 2 ins. in rib of k2, p2.

Next row.—K1, k2 tog. all along row so that 36 sts. rem. *Next row.*—P2, make 1, p2 tog. all along row. Work 3 rows in st.-st. *Next row.*—K17, make 1 in each of the next 2 sts., k17 (38 sts. on needle). *Next row.*—P.

Now work 20 rows in st.-st., increasing 1 st. in the 18th st. of each k. row, so that there are then 48 sts. on needle.

On the next plain row k18, then work 8 rows on the next 12 sts. to form the thumb. K2 tog. 6 times, break off wool, thread through these 6 sts., draw up, and sew sides of thumb-seam together.

Join wool on again at beg. of row, k18, pick up 2 sts. from base of thumb, k. rem. 18 sts. P. back 38 sts., then k. 10 rows in st.-st.

Next row.—K2, k2 tog. all along row, finishing with k2. Work 3 rows in st.-st.

Next row.—K1, k2 tog. all along row, finishing with k2. *Next row.*—P. *Next row.*—K2 tog. all along row.

Break off wool, thread it through the rem. sts., then press and sew up seam. Thread ribbon through holes at wrist.

A WRAPOVER VEST

Materials.—1½ ozs. 3-ply white wool ; 1 pair No. 8 knitting needles.

Measurements.—Length, 10 ins.

Commencing at the back, cast on 44 sts. K. 8 rows plain, then change to st.-st. and continue in st.-st. for 9 ins., finishing at a p. row. K. 12 sts., cast off 20 sts. for neck, then k. the last 12 sts. Turn, and p. 12 sts., then cast on 20 sts. for left front. Keeping 4 sts. at the front edge in garter-stitch, and the rest of the work in st.-st., continue working on these 32 sts. for 9 ins. Work 8 rows plain, and cast off.

Work the right front in the same manner as the left, casting on another 20 sts. to the 12 left for the shoulder.

THE SLEEVES.—Cast on 32 sts., and k. 8 rows plain. Change to st.-st. and inc. 1 st. at the beg. and end of every 4th row until there are 44 sts. on the needle. Continue until work measures 5 ins., then cast off loosely. Knit another sleeve to match.

Sew up side-seams and sleeves, stitch sleeves into arm-holes, and press.

WOOLLIES FOR THE OLDER CHILD

THE mother who can knit will find the problem of keeping up with the growing child in the matter of clothes considerably lightened, as well as the labour of keeping the clothes clean. A knitted pullover can be made for the price of a shirt, but two or three shirts that wanted constant washing would be worn out during the life of a pullover. So make a point of including some knitted garments in your children's wardrobe, for the cooler days.

A PAIR OF FINGERLESS GLOVES

Materials.—1 oz. 4-ply wool in natural ; 1 oz. 4-ply wool in scarlet ; 2 No. 8 knitting needles ; 4 No. 10 needles (points both ends) ; a crochet hook.

LEFT HAND.—With No. 8 needles and scarlet wool, cast on 64 sts. and work in k1, p1 rib for 1 in. Change to natural wool and continue in k1, p1 rib for 2½ ins. (3½ ins. in all).

Next row.—Change to No. 10 needles. *K1, p1, k2 tog., p1, k1, k2 tog., rep. from * to end (48 sts.). Work 3 rows in k1, p1 rib, then in the next row make holes for the cord thus :

*Rib 2, make 1, p2 tog., rep. from * to end. Work 3 rows more in k1, p1 rib. Now divide the sts. on to 3 No. 10 needles as follows : *1st needle.*—K12. *2nd needle.*—K24. *3rd needle.*—K12. Using a 4th needle, k. 9 rounds plain.

Next round.—K5, k. the next 7 sts. from the 1st needle, place them on a safety-pin, and leave them there for the thumb. K. to end of round.

Next round.—K5, cast off 7 sts., k. to end. K. 18 more rounds, then shape the top thus :

Next round.—1st needle.—K. to last 3 sts., k2 tog., k1. *2nd needle.*—K1, k2 tog. through the back of the loops, k. to the last 3 sts., k2 tog., k1. *3rd needle.*—K1, k2 tog. through back of loops, k. to end.

Next round.—K. Rep. the last 2 rounds until 16 sts. rem. (4, 8, 4). Break off wool and thread the end through the rem. sts. Draw up and fasten off.

THE THUMB.—Slip the 7 sts. from the safety-pin on to a No. 10 needle, then pick up the 7 cast-off sts. on to 2 No. 10 needles, and work 14 rounds.

Next round.—K2 tog. all round. *Next round.*—K1, * k2 tog., rep. from * all round.

Break off wool, thread through rem. sts. and fasten off. Work the right-hand glove in the same manner, slipping the first 7 sts. from the 3rd needle for the thumb instead of the last 7 sts. of the 1st needle. Crochet chain cords in scarlet for the wrists, attaching a small tassel at each end of the cord.

A PULLOVER FOR BOY OR GIRL

This pullover is suitable for a boy or girl from 8 to 10 years old. To make the pullover for an older child, measure the child according to the measurements given in the instructions, and cast on the extra number of stitches to fit. Alternately use a size larger needles to make the pullover fit a bigger child. It is easier to use needles a size larger if the child is only a little bigger than the measurements given. If, however, extra stitches are to be cast on, they should be 7 extra, or for a size 2 ins. larger, 14 extra, and so on in multiples of seven.

Materials.—7 ozs. 4-ply knitting wool in natural ; 1 oz. 4-ply wool in navy blue ; 1 pair No. 8 needles ; 4 No. 10 needles, pointed at both ends.

Measurements.—Length from shoulder to lower edges, 16 ins. ; chest, 27 ins. ; sleeve-seam (with cuff turned back), 14½ ins.

Tension.—On No. 8 needles, 6 sts. to 1 in.

THE FRONT.—Using No. 10 needles and navy blue wool, cast on 84 sts. Work 2 rows in k1, p1 rib. Change to natural wool and k. 1 row. Now continue in the k1, p1 rib until the work measures 2½ ins. from commencement, ending with a row on the wrong side of the work.

Change to No. 8 needles. Continue working in st.-st. (k. 1 row, p. 1 row) until the work measures 11 ins. from lower edge, ending with a p. row.

TO SHAPE THE ARM-HOLE.—Continue in st.-st., cast off 4 sts. at the beg. of the next 2 rows, then dec. 1 st. at each end of every row until 66 sts. rem. Now proceed without shaping until the work measures 15 ins. from lower edge, ending with a p. row.

SHAPE THE NECK AND SHOULDERS.—*Next row.*—K25, turn. Leave the rem. 41 sts. on a spare needle. Work on these 25 sts. as follows : *1st row.*—Cast off 2 sts., p. to end. *2nd row.*—K. to last 2 sts., k2 tog. *3rd row.*—P2 tog., p. to end. Rep. these last 2 rows once. *6th row.*—As 2nd row. *Next 3 rows.*—Work in st.-st. *10th row.*—Cast off 6, k. to end. *11th row.*—P. to end. Rep. these last 2 rows once. Cast off 6 sts.

Leave the centre 16 sts. on the spare needle and transfer the rem. 25 sts. on to a No. 8 needle with the point to the inner edge. Re-join wool and work to correspond with the first shoulder, substituting k. rows where p. rows are stated, and p. rows for k. rows.

THE BACK.—Work this exactly as given for the front until the arm-hole shapings are completed and 66 sts. rem. Now continue in st.-st. without shaping until the work measures 16 ins. from lower edge, ending with a p. row.

SHAPE THE NECK AND SHOULDERS.—*Next row.*—K24, turn. Leave remaining 42 sts. on a spare needle. Work on these 24 sts. as follows : *1st row.*—Cast off 2, p. to end. *2nd row.*—Cast off 6, k. to last 2 sts., k2 tog. *3rd row.*—P2 tog., p. to end.

Rep. these last 2 rows once. Cast off 6 sts. Leave the centre 18 sts. on the spare needle and transfer the rem. 24 sts. on to a No. 8 needle with the point to the inner edge. Re-join wool and work to correspond with the first shoulder, substituting k. rows where p. rows are stated, and p. rows for k. rows.

THE SLEEVES.—Using 2 No. 10 needles and navy blue wool, cast on 42 sts. Work 2 rows in k1, p1 rib. Change to natural wool and k. 1 row. Now continue in the rib until the work measures 4 ins. from commencement, ending with a row on the right side of the work. Change to No. 8 needles and work 6 rows in st.-st., commencing with a k. row to reverse the turn-back cuff. Continue in st.-st., inc. 1 st. each end of the next row, then each end of every following 10th row until 60 sts. are on the needle. Now proceed without shaping until the work measures 16½ ins. from lower edge, ending with a p. row.

To SHAPE THE TOP.—Continue in st.-st., dec. 1 st. both ends of each of the next 2 rows, then work 1 row without shaping. Rep. these last 3 rows until 20 sts. rem. Cast off.

THE COLLAR.—Join the back and front shoulder-seams. With the right side of the work facing you, and using the 4 No. 10 needles and natural wool, commence at the left shoulder and work as follows : pick up and k. 22 sts. along the front neck edge, 16 sts. from the spare needle, 22 sts. along the neck edge to the right shoulder, 13 sts. along the back neck edge, 18 sts. from the spare needle, 13 sts. along the neck edge to the left shoulder (104 sts.). Arrange these sts. on the 3 needles, 34 on each of 2 needles and 36 on the 3rd needle, and work in rounds of k1, p1 rib for 3¾ ins. Change to the navy blue wool and p. 1 row. Work 2 rows in rib, then cast off loosely in rib. Make up in the usual way.

FOR A WOMAN'S WARDROBE

APART from the additional scope for turning out attractive garments, there is no more effective method of keeping down dress bills than for a woman to knit her own woollies. Not only are home-made knitted garments so much cheaper to make in the first place, but they last about three times as long as bought ones and, with careful washing,[1] look nice to the last. Here are some patterns for garments which would make a useful addition to any woman's wardrobe.

[1] See p. 11.

LADY'S GLOVES

This is a most attractive pair of gloves, worked in moss-stitch.

Materials.—2 ozs. 4-ply fingering ; 4 No. 12 needles with double points.

RIGHT-HAND GLOVE.—Cast on 48 sts. on 3 needles (16, 16, 16) and work in rounds of rib of k1, p1 for 3½ ins. Dec. 1 st. at end of last round. *Next round.*—Inc., inc., m.-s. to end of round. *Next 2 rounds.*—M.-s. *Next round.*—Inc., m.-s. 2, inc., m.-s. to end. *Next 2 rounds.*—M.-s. *Next round.*—Inc., m.-s. 4, inc., m.-s. to end. *Next 2 rounds.*—M.-s. *Next round.*—Inc., M.-s. 6, inc., m.-s. to end. *Next 2 rounds.*—M.-s. *Next round.*—Inc., m.-s. 8, inc., m.-s. to end. *Next 2 rounds.*—M.-s. *Next round.*—Inc., m.-s. 10, inc., m.-s. to end. *Next 2 rounds.*—M.-s. *Next round.*—Inc., m.-s. 12, inc., m.-s. to end. *Next 2 rounds.*—M.-s. *Next round.*—Inc., m.-s. 14, inc., m.-s. to end. *Next 2 rounds.*—M.-s. *Next round.*—Inc., m.-s. 16, inc., m.-s. to end. *Next 2 rounds.*—M.-s. *Next round.*— Inc., m.-s. 18, m.-s. to end. *Next 2 rounds.*—M.-s. *Next round.*— M.-s. 1, slip the next 19 sts. on piece of wool for thumb, cast on 3, m.-s. to end (51 sts.). Work 19 rounds m.-s.

1ST FINGER.—M.-s. 4, slip all but the last 9 sts. on to a piece of wool, cast on 2, m.-s. last 9 sts. Work in rounds of m.-s. for 30 rounds.

Next round.—K2 tog., k1 to end of round. Break off wool, thread a darning needle and draw up sts. Fasten off securely.

2ND FINGER.—M.-s. the next 7 sts. from wool, cast on 3, m.-s. last 7 sts. from wool, pick up and k2 from base of previous finger. Work in m.-s. for 34 rounds. Finish as for 1st finger.

3RD FINGER.—M.-s. the next 6 sts. from wool, cast on 2, m.-s. the last 6 sts. from wool, pick up and k. 3 sts. from base of previous finger. Work in m.-s. for 30 rounds. Finish as for 1st finger.

4TH FINGER.—M.-s. rem. 12 sts. from wool, pick up and k. 3 sts. from base of previous finger. Work in m.-s. for 26 rounds. Finish as for 1st finger.

THUMB.—M.-s. 19 sts. from wool, pick up and k. 4 sts. from base of hand, work in m.-s. for 28 rounds. Finish as for 1st finger.

LEFT-HAND GLOVE.—Work as for right-hand glove as far as 1st finger. M.-s. 13, slip the rem. sts. on to piece of wool, cast on 2. Arrange on 3 needles and finish as for 1st finger of right glove. Now continue from 2nd finger of right-hand glove to end.

NOTE.—These gloves can be made in st.-st. by following the instructions above, but knitting every round plain instead of m.-s. If st.-st. is used, keep an even number of sts. throughout, except the 19 sts. for the thumb.

SLIPOVER JUMPER AND ANKLE SOCKS

This jumper and the socks are simple to make and delightful to wear. The countrywoman in particular will find them useful for many occasions.

Materials.—8 ozs. Shetland or fine 4-ply wool for the slipover and 2 oz. for the socks ; 2 No. 9 and 4 No. 12 needles, the latter pointed at both ends.

Measurements.—Slipover : length, 23 ins. ; bust, 34-36 ins. Socks : foot, 9½ ins. (adjustable).

Tension.—Using No. 9 needles, about 8 sts. to 1 in., measured over slightly-stretched pattern.

THE SLIPOVER

FRONT.—Using No. 9 needles, cast on 148 sts. and work in the following pattern :

1st row.—*K1, p2, k1, p4, k6, p4, k1, p2. Rep. from * to last st., k1.

2nd row.—P1, *k2, p1, k4, p6, k4, p1, k2, p1. Rep. from * to end.

3rd-6th rows.—Rep. 1st-2nd rows twice.

7th row.—*K1, p2, k1, p1, slip next 3 sts. on to a spare needle and leave at back of work, k. next 2 sts., then p. 3 sts. from spare needle, k2, s. next 2 sts. on to a spare needle and leave at front of work, p. next 3 sts., then k2 sts. from spare needle, p1, k1, p2. Rep. from * to last st., k1.

8th row.—P1, *k2, p1, k1, p2, k3, p2, k3, p2, k1, p1, k2, p1. Rep. from * to end.

These eight rows form the pattern.

Beginning again from the 1st row, continue in pattern until work measures 4 ins. from commencement.

Change to No. 12 needles and continue in pattern for 1½ ins., ending with a row on wrong side of work.

Next row.—*K1, p2 tog., k1, pattern 14 sts., k1, p2 tog. Rep. from * to last st., k1.

Next row.—P1, *k1, p1, pattern 14 sts., p1, k1, p1. Rep. from * to end of row.

Next row.—*K1, p1, k1, pattern 14 sts., k1, p1. Rep. from * to last st., k1. Rep. these 2 rows for 2 ins., ending with a row on wrong side of work.

Next row.—*K1, p. twice into next st., k1, pattern 14 sts., k1, p. twice into next st. Rep. from * to last st., k1.

Continue in pattern until work measures 9 ins. from lower edge. Change to No. 9 needles and continue in pattern until work measures 16 ins. from lower edge.

SHAPE ARM-HOLE AND DIVIDE FOR NECK OPENING.—Keeping the continuity of the pattern, cast off 11 sts. at the beg. of the next 2 rows, then dec. 1 st. at both ends of the next 10 rows.

Next row.—Pattern across 53 sts., turn, and leave rem. 53 sts. on a spare needle. Continue in pattern on these 53 sts., dec. 1 st. at neck edge on every alternate row until 30 sts. rem. Proceed without shaping until work measures 23½ ins. from lower edge, ending at arm-hole edge.

TO SHAPE SHOULDER.—*Next row.*—Cast off 10 sts., work to end of row. *Next row.*—Work to end. Rep. these 2 rows once. Cast off rem. sts.

Re-join wool at neck edge of rem. sts. and work this side to correspond.

THE BACK.—Using No. 9 needles, cast on 137 sts. and work in rib thus :

1st row.—*P2, k1. Rep. from * to last 2 sts., p2. *2nd row.*—*K2, p1. Rep. from * to last 2 sts., k2. Rep. these 2 rows for 4 ins.

Change to No. 12 needles and continue in rib for 1½ ins., ending with a row on wrong side of work.

Next row.—*P2 tog., k1. Rep. from * to last 2 sts., p2 tog.

Next row.—*K1, p1. Rep. from * to last st., k1.

Next row.—*P1, k1. Rep. from * to last st., p1.

Rep. these 2 rows for 2 ins., ending with a row on wrong side of work.

Next row.—*P. twice into next st., k1. Rep. from * to last st. P. twice into next st.

Continue in P2, k1 rib until work measures 9 ins. from lower edge. Change to No. 9 needles and continue in rib until work measures 16 ins. from lower edge.

TO SHAPE ARM-HOLES.—Continuing in rib, cast off 10 sts. at beg. of next 2 rows, then dec. 1 st. at both ends of every row until 97 sts. rem.

Proceed without shaping until work measures 22½ ins. from lower edge, ending with a row on wrong side of work.

TO SHAPE SHOULDERS.—Cast off 10 sts. at beg. of next 4 rows, then cast off 8 sts. at beg. of next 2 rows.

Cast off remaining sts. for back of neck.

THE NECK BAND.—Using No. 12 needles, cast on 12 sts. and work in k1, p1 rib until band is long enough to fit round neck edge when slightly stretched. Cast off.

THE ARM-HOLE BANDS (2 PIECES).—Using No. 12 needles, cast on 12 sts. and work in k1, p1 rib until band is long enough to fit all round arm-hole edge when slightly stretched. Cast off.

TO MAKE UP.—Press the work lightly on wrong side, taking care not to stretch the fabric. Join shoulder-seams. Stitch arm-hole bands along arm-hole edges, then fold over on to right side and stitch down again. Join side-seams. Stitch neck band round neck edge to match arm-hole bands, easing it round the point of the neck. Press all seams.

THE ANKLE SOCKS

Made by themselves, the socks take 2 ozs. wool.

Using No. 12 needles, cast on 68 sts. and work thus :

1st row.—K1, p1, *k1, p2, k1, p4, k6, p4, k1, p2. Rep. from * to last 3 sts., k1, p2. *2nd row.*—K2, *p1, k1, p1, k4, p6, k4, p1, k2. Rep. from * to last 3 sts., p1, k2. Rep. these 2 rows twice.

7th row.—K1, p1, *k1, p2, k1, p1, s. next 3 sts. to a spare needle and leave at back of work, k. next 2 sts., then p. 3 sts. from spare needle, k2, s. next 2 sts. on to a spare needle and leave at front of work, p. next 3 sts., then k. 2 sts. from spare needle, p1, k1, p2. Rep. from * to last 3 sts., k1, p2.

8th row.—K2, *p1, k2, p1, k1, p2, k3, p2, k3, p2, k1, p1, k2. Rep. from * to last 3 sts., p1, k2.

These 8 rows form the pattern. Rep. them until the work measures 3 ins. from commencement.

Next row.—Pattern across 49 sts., turn. *Next row.*—Pattern 30 sts., turn.

Continue in pattern on these 30 sts., always knitting the 2 edge sts., until work measures 8½ ins. from commencement, ending with a row on wrong side of work.

SHAPE TOE.—*1st row.*—K1, k2 tog., k. to last 3 sts., k2 tog., k1. *2nd row.*—P. to end.

Rep. these 2 rows until 10 sts. rem. Leave these sts. on a spare needle. Return to rem. sts. and place these on to 1 needle for the heel, with the back-seam in centre of needle. Work thus : *1st row.*—*S1, k1. Rep. from * to end. *2nd row.*—P. to end. Rep. these 2 rows 12 times.

To TURN THE HEEL.—*1st row.*—K23, k2 tog., turn. *2nd row.*—P9, p2 tog., turn. *3rd row.*—K9, k2 tog., turn. Rep. last 2 rows until all side sts. are worked off and 10 sts. rem., finishing at the end of a p. row. *Next row.*—K10, pick up and k. 14 sts. down side of heel-flap, turn. *Next row.*—P24, pick up and p. 14 sts. down side of heel-flap.

SHAPE INSTEP.—*1st row.*—K1, k2 tog., k. to last 3 sts., k2 tog., k1. *Next row.*—P. to end.

Rep. last 2 rows until 30 sts. rem.

Proceed without shaping until work measures same as top of foot to toe, ending with a p. row.

Shape toe as given for top of foot, then graft, or cast off the two sets of sts. together.

To MAKE UP.—Press work lightly on wrong side, using a hot iron over a damp cloth. Join leg and foot seams and press.

A VEST AND PANTIE SET

Materials.—6 ozs. of 2-ply wool, 3 ozs. for each garment ; 2 No. 8 and 2 No. 12 knitting needles ; a medium-sized crochet hook ; 1 yard of ribbon ; about ¾ yard of elastic braid, 5 to 7 holes in width. If the braid is unobtainable, use tight ribbing, 3 or 4 inches wide, for the foundation.

Measurements.—Vest : length, 25 ins. (excluding points) ; bust, 32-36 ins. Panties : length from waist to leg edge, 15 ins. *Tension.*—With No. 8 needles, 1 pattern measures about 2 ins. when slightly stretched.

THE TRUNKS

FRONT.—With No. 12 needles and double wool, begin about ¾ in. from one end of the elastic braid and pick up and k. 1 st. into each of the next 78 holes. Break off 1 thread of wool, turn, and continue in single wool.

Next row.—*K1, p1, inc. in next st. Rep. from * to end (104 sts.). Now continue in k1, p1 rib, inc. 1 st. at both ends of the 7th and every following 8th row, until 134 sts. are on the needle. Continue in rib without further shaping until work measures 10 ins. from the commencement (excluding the braid), and ending with a row on the wrong side. Now begin the gusset :

1st row.—Rib 66, k. twice into each of the next 2 sts., rib to end. *2nd row.*—Rib 66, p4, rib to end. *3rd row.*—Rib 66, k. twice into next st., k2, k. twice into next st., rib to end. *4th row.*—Rib 66, p6, rib to end. *5th row.*—Rib 66, k. twice into next st., k4, k. twice into next st., rib to end.

Continue thus, keeping the gusset sts. in st.-st. and the sts. on each side in rib, and inc. 1 st. after the first 66 sts. and before the last 66 sts. until 158 sts. are on the needle.

Next row.—Rib 66, p. to last 66 sts., rib to end. *Next row.*—Rib 66, cast off 66 sts. in rib, rib to end. Work 1 in. in rib on these last 66 sts., then cast off. Rejoin wool and work 1 in. in rib on rem. 66 sts., then cast off.

THE BACK.—Using the wool double, pick up and k. 1 st. into each of the next 78 holes in the braid, leaving at least ¾ in. turning at the other end. Break off 1 thread of wool and inc. as given for the front to 104 sts.

SHAPE THE BACK.—*1st row.*—Rib 59, turn. *2nd row.*—Rib 14, turn. *3rd row.*—Rib 19, turn. *4th row.*—Rib 24, turn. *5th row.*—Rib 29, turn. Continue in this manner, taking up 5 extra sts. on every row until all the sts. are worked on to one needle. Now continue to match the front.

TO MAKE UP.—Press the work very lightly on the wrong side, taking care not to stretch the ribbing. Join side, leg and gusset seams, and stitch the elastic braid together, turning under the ends of the braid and stitching down neatly. Press the seams, using a warm iron over a damp cloth.

THE VEST

THE FRONT.—With No. 8 needles, begin at the bottom and cast on 113 sts. and work in pattern thus :

1st row.—K1, p1, k1, p2, k1, wl. fwd., s1, k2 tog., p.s.s.o., wl. fwd., k1, p2, *k1 (p1, k1) twice, p2, k1, wl. fwd., s1, k2 tog., p.s.s.o., wl. fwd., k1, p2. Rep. from * to the last 3 sts., k1, p1, k1.

2nd row.—P1, k1, p1, k2, p5, k2, *p1 (k1, p1) twice, k2, p5, k2. Rep. from * to last 3 sts., p1, k1, p1.

3rd row.—K1, p1, k1, p2, k5, p2, *k1 (p1, k1) twice, p2, k5, p2. Rep. from * to last 3 sts., k1, p1, k1.

4th row.—P1, k1, p1, k2, p5, k2, *p1 (k1, p1) twice, k2, p5, k2. Rep. from * to last 3 sts., p1, k1, p1.

These 4 rows form the pattern. Rep. them until work measures 14 ins., ending with a row on the wrong side. Change to No. 12 needles.

Next row.—*K3, k2 tog., k3. Rep. from * to last st., k1 (99 sts.).

Next row.—S1, *k1, p1. Rep. from * to end.

Next row.—*K1, p1. Rep. from * to last st., k1.

Rep. last 2 rows for 5 ins. Change to No. 8 needles and continue in pattern as given for lower part of vest for a further 6 ins.

**To SHAPE TOP.—*Next row.*—Work 45 sts., cast off 9 sts., work to end. Working on last set of 45 sts., and keeping pattern correct, k2 tog. at both ends of every row until 3 sts. rem. K3 tog. Break off wool and fasten off. Rejoin wool at needle-point and work to match first side.

BACK.—Work to match front as far as ** then cast off.

To MAKE UP.—Press the work very lightly on the wrong side, taking care not to stretch the ribbing. Sew up side-seams. Using the crochet hook, work the following picot edge round the top : 1 single crochet into the first st., *3 chain, 1 double crochet into the first of these chains, miss 1 st. of foundation, 1 single crochet into next. Rep. from * all round. Sew on shoulder-straps, and press seams and crochet edging.

A B C OF SEWING TERMS

Back-stitch.—This is a stitch made by hand to look like machine-stitching, and it gives the same strength. It is done by bringing the needle up from the wrong side of the material, then inserting it again close to the point where it was brought through and taking a small stitch forward. The needle is then put in again where this stitch started to make a stitch on the wrong side of the material twice as long as the first stitch on the right side. The needle is then inserted again where the first stitch ended, and a second long stitch taken on the wrong side. Back-stitch is a good stitch to use for heavy seams, or on any sewing where a firm stitch is needed.

Basting.—This is an American term for tacking.

Bias.—A term that indicates material cut on the cross. Bias bindings and bias strips are used to edge any curved line such as neck-lines, or the hem of a skirt which has been cut on the cross. To cut a true bias, measure across a piece of material diagonally so that the line falls exactly between the lengthwise and crosswise threads of your fabric.

Blanket-stitch.—This stitch is used to neaten raw edges, and is especially suitable for heavy materials, and for repairing the edges of fraying carpets, rugs and blankets. It is worked from left to right, and is like an open buttonhole-stitch.

Buttonhole-stitch.—This stitch is used for buttonholes, sometimes to appliqué materials one on to another, and in scalloping. To do buttonhole-stitching, hold the work towards you and insert the needle at the back of the fabric at the left and draw through. Then hold the thread flat with the left thumb, put the needle in again over the fabric, bringing it out just below the thread you're holding, and draw the thread through over it.

Couching-stitch.—This stitch is used in securing two or more threads flatly to material by taking stitches across them to hold them down. The stitches that hold them down can be worked either straight or on the slant, but should be small and made at even distances from each other.

Feather-stitch.—This stitch is used to decorate children's garments and lingerie. It is worked like buttonhole-stitch except that the stitches are perpendicular instead of horizontal. Bring the needle through from the wrong side at the top of the line you are working, then, holding the thread down with the left thumb, take a slanting stitch a little lower down, bringing the needle through over the thread you are holding. Repeat till the whole line is worked.

Felling.—Another term for hemming. It is done rather more rapidly, with larger stitches and longer distances between the stitches than hemming, but the principle is the same.

Flat Fell-seam.—A method of joining seams, which is more commonly known as seam and fell, or running and felling. It is made by placing the two edges of material right sides facing, and with one edge about a quarter of an inch below the other. Work along the lower edge, close to the edge with small running-stitches. Then open the seam out flat, and turn the top edge under, hemming it down flat over the running-stitches.

Gauging.—The term used for several rows of gathering threads one beneath the other. All the rows are worked with running-stitches, as evenly as possible beneath each other. The ends are left loose, and then all drawn up together when the requisite number of rows are completed.

Hemming.—This is used to fasten down raw edges, and should be done with fairly small, very regular stitches. The edge of the material is first folded over to bring the raw edge on the wrong side, and then the raw edge is itself folded in and concealed. The needle is inserted under the top of the folded edge of the material, brought down, and a tiny stitch taken beneath the fold. The needle is then pushed up into the top edge, which is lightly caught, and then brought down again to take another small stitch.

Herring-boning.—This is done on flannel or light woven materials to fasten down hems or raw edges where the material is too thick to turn under double and hem. It is worked by drawing two parallel lines, and inserting the needle in the lower line at the left. With the needle pointing left, bring the thread up and put a small stitch in the top line to the right. Go back to the lower line again, and with the needle still pointing left, put in another stitch to the right of the one just made at the top. Then up again and to the right, and down again till the line is filled.

Lapped Seam.—A lapped seam is a seam joining two pieces of material on the right side. It is used for raglan sleeves sometimes, and to set the yoke of a dress on to the bodice. One raw edge of the material is turned under, and tacked on top of the other flat raw edge. It is then stitched with small fine stitches, close together, on the right side.

Overcasting.—This stitch is also known as oversewing. It is a stitch used to neaten raw edges and stop them from fraying, or to seam together suède or stiff fabrics that will not press flat, or double under for ordinary seaming and felling. It should be done loosely on raw edges, but rather more tightly when it is used to join materials. It is worked over the edge of the material from left to right.

Piping.—This is a way of finishing off straight or curved edges to give them a professional look. It is used on the edges of cushions, coats, and some dress-seams. It is done by covering a length of cord with self-material, putting this between the two pieces of material that are to be seamed, and stitching the four thicknesses of material together.

Raglan.—A term used for a semi-fitted sleeve which has a seam down the centre of the sleeve, and the sleeve and bodice edges joined together in the shoulder-seams. This type of sleeve, being loosely fitted, is used mostly on overcoats, kimono-type dressing-gowns, and children's frocks and coats.

Ruching.—A trimming made by cutting strips of material on the cross and gathering them at the edges to make frills. It is used chiefly to trim the necks and wrist edges of garments.

Running.—A small stitch made for gathers, for seaming, or for tucks. It is the simplest of all sewing processes. The needle is pushed in and out of the material, taking up only a tiny piece of the material each time.

Satin-stitch.—This is the simplest of embroidery stitches. It is done by working the thread over the space to be filled so that each separate thread lies alongside the next one close together. You simply make straight stitches from one edge of your outline to the other edge, bringing out the needle and thread for the next stitch as close as possible to where you inserted it for the first stitch. The stitches must be kept very smooth and even. Satin-stitch is often used to join lace flat to neck-lines.

Scalloping.—A finish for raw edges, especially neck edges. It is usually worked from a transfer, but scallops can be outlined on the edge of a garment with a coin, a penny or halfpenny, according to the size of scallop you wish to produce. Scalloping is much used on the edges of babies' garments. It is done like a close buttonhole-stitch, the scallops being padded first with close running-stitches or with chain-stitch to raise them and make them firmer.

Shirring.—An American term for gathering.

Slip-stitching.—This is like a wide hemming, and is used to turn up the bottom of coats and dresses where the stitches should not be brought through on to the right side of the garment. It is also used to attach linings to garments, and to sew on neck and wrist trimmings. It is done by picking up a very few threads of the material on the needle just below the top fold to be stitched down, and then passing the needle along under the fold for about a quarter of an inch before it is put into the top of the material.

Smocking.—A form of embroidery over gathers, to hold them together and form a design. The gathers are made from a transfer of small pin dots, each gather being picked up exactly on the point of the dot. When the lines have all been gathered, the gathers are held together by lines of feather-stitching, or simple bar-stitch to form a honeycomb pattern. Smocking is particularly attractive on the clothes of young children. It should be done on materials that are not too thick, otherwise the effect is clumsy and bulky.

Stab-stitch.—This is used for very thick materials where the stitch cannot be picked up on the needle and the thread drawn straight through. It is like back-stitching, only the needle is pushed in, pulled through, pushed up again and pulled through.

Tacking.—Tacking is used to hold seam edges and all sewing together before it is finally stitched. Special tacking cotton is sold for this purpose, as large stitches are made and this cotton does not twist or mark the material. Insert the needle into the material and bring it out about half-an-inch along. Pass over a quarter-of-an-inch, insert the needle again, and bring it out after another half-an-inch.

Tailor's Tacks.—These tacks are used to mark the lines of seams on garments, where chalk marks are not enough. They are made by picking up a couple of stitches with the needle about a-quarter-of-an-inch long, and using a double thread. A space is left of about a quarter-of-an-inch, then two more stitches picked up, leaving behind loops big enough to get your first finger through. The loops are later snipped, and leave behind a line of threads to mark the position of perforations in the pattern, or unusual seams. Where pleats have to be placed exactly one over the other, or any seam directly above the other, tailor's tacks are used on double material to mark these places exactly. The top layer of material is carefully pulled up inch by inch, and the threads snipped between the two layers.

Tucks.—A decorative way of taking up fullness in garments, at the shoulders, waist-lines, etc. Tucks are made on the right side of the garment when used as a trimming, and consist of a tiny pleat of material fixed into place with small running-stitches, preferably done by hand. On thick materials tucks may be machine-stitched. Their beauty depends on keeping them even and an equal distance apart. To do this, use a cardboard gauge when tacking them up. You can make the gauge yourself from any piece of thin cardboard by cutting notches in it to give you the width of tuck you want.

Welt.—This term usually denotes ribbing, either to make a sock fit closely at the top or a knitted jumper fit snugly at the waist and hips in knitting. It also means a special kind of seam used on men's and boys' clothes. It is made on the right side like a lapped-seam, only the machining is worked about an eighth-of-an-inch from the turned-under edge, thus forming a kind of raised effect on the right side of the garment. Two lines of machine-stitching are often made for strength. Pockets are sometimes attached to a coat this way, and are then known as welt pockets.

Whipping.—This is used to gather lace and delicate frills on to garments. It is done by rolling the edge of the fabric between the left thumb and forefinger very tightly then, with the needle pointing towards you at the top of the roll, it is inserted just beneath it, taken through to the back, and the thread brought down over the roll.

INDEX AND
PRONOUNCING GLOSSARY

HOW TO USE THIS INDEX.—In order to facilitate immediate reference to the principal entry on a particular subject, the page number for this entry is set in italics, thus: *158*. Subsidiary references to the subject which occur elsewhere in the book are indicated by numerals in roman type, thus: 167. References to line drawings are printed in roman type and enclosed in square brackets, thus: [31]. Cross references given in the index refer only to the index pages.

THE PRONOUNCING GLOSSARY.—Where the pronunciation of names and technical terms is not immediately understood from the spelling, or where the spelling may be misleading, a complete phonetic re-spelling is given after the first index entry. The word is broken into syllables as it is spoken, and an accent mark (′) follows the syllable on which the stress is placed. The notation used for the phonetic re-spelling is as follows:

ā	*ma*te	a	p*a*t	è	th*e*re	th	*th*in
ē	m*e*te	e	p*e*t	a	f*a*ther	TH	*th*ine
ī	m*i*te	i	p*i*t	ę	h*er*	zh	lei*s*ure
ō	m*o*te	o	p*o*t	aw	*aw*l	ch	*ch*urch
ū	m*u*te	u	n*u*t	oi	*oi*l	g	*g*et
ōō	b*oo*t	oo	f*oo*t	ow	*ow*l	j	*j*am

The French nasalised n is denoted by italicising the vowel and the nasal concerned, thus: u*n*, bo*n*, vi*n*.

ABBREVIATIONS, knitting, 94.
Accessories, to choose, 57-58.
— to make, 58-62.
— to make from pieces, 61-62.
Ankle socks, to knit, 107, *109*.
Aprons from cotton frocks, 70.
Arm, to measure, 22.
Arm-hole, to measure, 22.
Army, comforts for, 94-99.
Arrow-headed pleat, 56.
Artificial silk, to iron, 11.

BABY'S BONNET, to knit, 99-100.
— bootees, to knit, 100.
— clothes, to choose, 76-77.
— — to make, 76-79.
— leggings, to knit, 100-102.
— matinée jacket, 78.
— mittens, to knit, 102.
— nightdress, to make, 77.
— petticoat, to make, 76-77.
— vests, to choose, 76.
— — to knit, 102.
Back-stitch, [33], 112.
Balaclava (bal-a-klá′va) helmet, to knit, 95.
Basting, 112.
Bell sleeves, 47.

Belt, to make, 37, 62.
Belts, materials for, 13.
— to trim, 60-61.
Benzine, use of, 9.
Beret, to make, 89-90.
Bias, meaning of, 112.
Bias-cut lingerie, to iron, 21.
Binding buttonholes, 54-55.
— false, 51-52.
— lingerie, 28.
— neck-lines, 36, 37.
— seams, 47-48.
Black clothes, to restore, 10.
— glacé (glas′á) shoes, to clean, 8-9.
— kid shoes, to clean, 8-9.
Blanket-stitch, 112.
Block patterns, to make, 21-23, 39, 40.
Blouse, child's, to make, 80-81.
— from shirt, 70.
— in rationed wardrobe, 5.
— material for, 13.
— pattern for, 40.
— to save coupons on, 4.
Blouses, to choose, 2.
Bodice pattern, to make, 22-23.
Bolero (bo-lār′ō) from long coat, 68.
Bonnet, baby's, to knit, 99-100.
Bootees, to knit, 100.

117